Praise for Coach Davies and Renegade Training

"In my 20 years of coaching, I have been fortunate to have been associated with a lot of top quality coaches. When I think of someone whom I would want to send my kids to for speed and quickness development along with a new approach to overall training methods, the one who comes to mind first and foremost is John Davies.

I have personally watched him interact on the field and have had the opportunity to send a lot of my athletes to him and everyone one of them have made incredible gains in all aspects.

John is unique with his style, he has cutting edge techniques, but what impresses me most is the way he puts things into a simplified and easy to understand methods that can be tailored to athletes at all levels.

Undoubtedly you will find John's *Renegade Training for Football* to be both rewarding and refreshing!! Enjoy!!"

—Steve Mooshagian, Wide Receiver Coach, Cincinnati Bengals

"I just wanted to thank you for all of the power-speed programs you have developed for our football program the past two years. We continue to make tremendous progress in the area of speed development and conditioning. The individual programs you have developed by position serves as a motivational tool for our players. Our players have responded well to the position specific training regiments. The blend of 100% sprint work with agility, interval training, resistance sprints, tempo sprints, GPP, SPP, and power-speed drills is truly outstanding. Adding the functional speed-strength work medicine ball drills and sand pit has given us a nice package to work with in developing a faster, powerful athlete. Our staff continues to be amazed at how well our players have progressed through the different levels of the power-speed program. The program emphasizes total athletic development while elevating work capacity and training volumes. The power-speed program demands the best from each player every day during the off-season and pre-season training period.

Thanks again John for all of your help. You have made an impact on the Clemson Strength, Speed and Conditioning staff and our football program. We look forward to working with you in the off-season. Best of Luck and Go Tigers!"

— Joey Batson, SCC, MSS, Director of Strength Speed and Conditioning, Clemson University

"Joining the Renegade Coaching program has made an immediate impact on the young athletes that I work with. As their personal coach I want the best for them. What better programs to give them than the Renegade Workout? GPP and its proper implementation have made me a believer in any program John Davies creates. I have seen dramatic changes in my athlete's hip flexibility and overall work capacity. Coach Davies training program has launched my athletes' confidence and will to succeed."

—Dan Fichter, Wannagetfast, Power Speed Training, Rochester, NY

"Playing football it Canada, you do not receive the same level of coaching that players do in the U.S., and are often left to fend for yourself when it comes to off-season training. Over the years I have tried nearly every 'football specific' workout out there, and found that none of them addressed all of the needs specific to the sport of football. However, Coach Davies' program addresses all of these needs—speed, agility, strength, power and general physical preparation—and puts them into a properly periodized and easy to follow year-round workout program. I have made incredible progress over a short period of time using his workouts, and wish that I had access to his guidance years ago."
—**Scott Vass**, Simon Fraser University Clansmen Football.

"John's work is on the cutting edge; it always has been and always will be. He dares to go where few will tread. He attacks athletic performance with a force firmly founded in tradition as well as venturing into what some deem unconventional. In the end, the results speak for themselves. Wins, wins, and more wins. Little more need be said."
— **Mike Ryan**, College and High School football coach, CA

"Coach Davies' concepts on training football players are the best that I have ever encountered! His "renegade style" of training the football athlete is unique to any other form of training. It does not emphasize just one or two aspects of football such as weight training and conditioning; it emphasizes all facets equally, which in turn creates a great player on the gridiron. Explosive strength, agility, quickness, flexibility, special awareness, reaction time, conditioning and most importantly, warrior attitude and mental & physical toughness are all developed fully and given equal attention!"
— **Derek Alford**, Offensive Coordinator/Quarterbacks, Garland High School, TX.

"John Davies is the new wizard of innovation in sport-specific training. If you don't read this book, then winning must not be very important to you."
—**Arik Orosz**, Trainer, Minneapolis, MN

"Our players are in the best shape they've ever been in and they're able to keep up with other teams who a year ago blew past them. The boys have a love/hate relationship with the program. They believe in it and are willing to go through it, but they also admit that it's the toughest thing they've ever done. They know it will make them better athletes as well as people. If you're gonna be a bear, be a grizzly."
— **Jabo Burgess**, Coach, Easley High School Easley, SC

"Working with Coach Davies was been the most intense experience in both the training and the results that I have had since starting training twenty years ago. I have become a true "Renegade." I now prefer to train alone after the gym closes by myself, leaving my training partners wondering what has caused my new found level of speed, strength and endurance."
— **Jay Cox**, Deputy Sheriff, Bishopville, MD

"I have learned more in seven months from Coach Davies about the practical application of exercises and hard work in the real world than I did from the other "experts" in 17 years lifting, a Master's degree in Exercise Physiology, countless journals and magazines."
— **Kevin Herring**, Birmingham, AL

"Coach Davies—One word: Loyal. This man has stuck with me and every other guy that he has come in contact. He has done it with vigilance and determination, to make us the BEST we can be. Everything that he has taught me has at one time or another seemed odd. But all of it, has been beneficial to not only me but to my athletes. Coach Davies over time has instilled a toughness that I have not had in years and through him I am able to pass that same toughness, that 'Never say die' attitude on to my players. When every other Coach has turned me down, he has found faith in me and given me the chance to be the BEST. He truly is a Coach among Coaches."
—**Jeff Olech**, Strength Coach, Boulder High School, Boulder, CO

"I wanted to take some time to thank you for the knowledge and insight that you have supplied us with in the last two years. I am amazed at the strides that the Defensive Line and Linebackers have made in the last two summers. My athletes' hip strength and explosiveness have improved tremendously from the Power Speed Drills and the Short Cone Drills that we have used.
Another amazing factor is the level of condition that my athletes have reached using your program. I am looking forward to seeing 100% of my athletes pass our conditioning test. Your Speed Program and you have been tremendous assets to Clemson Athletics and myself. The speed testing numbers from this summer were unbelievable and a great testament to your knowledge of speed training. I would recommend your program to any coach or athlete. You have changed my view of what sped training is all about. I am so excited about this program that I want to skip the season and start the third year of it today. I really appreciate everything that you have done for Clemson and our staff."
—**Russell Patterson**, SCCC, SSC, Assistant Strength Coach, Clemson University

"Most strength coaches and football athletes have confused football conditioning with weight lifting. The ability to bench press the weight room has little positive transfer to the playing arena. Fortunately, John Davies' new book on football conditioning will provide the proper roadmap for the aspiring football athlete and his strength coach. The depth of Coach Davies' experience with the football athlete combined with his in-depth knowledge is rarely found in today's contemporary coach. I have found him to be an invaluable resource. His workouts are not only a tremendous challenge that produces results, but they provide a refreshing perspective on this modern gizmo, no pain and no gain mentality. I would not hesitate to recommend this book to any athlete or conditioning consultant."
— **Michael Rutherford**, M.S. Exercise Physiology.

"All great coaches will agree that we must develop speed, strength, and conditioning in order for our athletes to be successful. John Davies has added the words, "Sport-specific", to my training philosophies in a meaningful way. With Coach Davies methods not only have I added depth and width to the body, but also to the mind of these athletes as we push beyond what was once thought to be the limit of their abilities both genetically and psychologically. The difference between the great coaches and John Davies is the "simple man" always willing to answer a question approach that he has with all of us that have been fortunate to cross paths with him. I will never get tired of listening to the "ramblings of this old coach", as it is always a learning experience!"

— Dale"Trouble"Wallace

"Coach Davies is the real deal. After three months of training under his guidance, I was able to reach levels of strength and speed that I never thought would've been possible. I'm much more confident in my skills as an athlete and can't wait to be able to apply them to the football field in a few months."

—M.J. Mafaro, Staten Island, NY.

RENEGADE TRAINING™ FOR FOOTBALL

COACH DAVIES

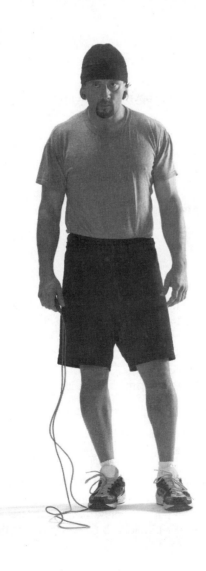

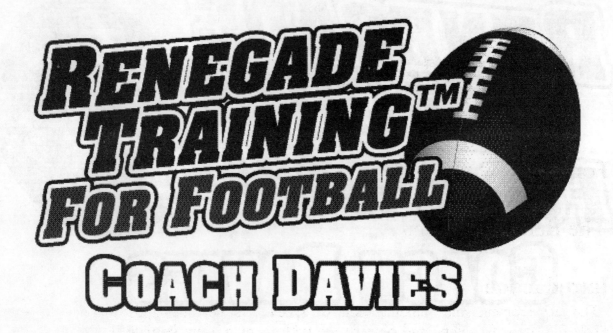

Published in the United States by:
Dragon Door Publications, Inc
P.O. Box 4381, St. Paul, MN 55104
Tel: (651) 487-2180 • Fax: (651) 487-3954
Credit card orders: 1-800-899-5111
Email: dragondoor@aol.com • Website: www.dragondoor.com

ISBN: 0-938045-42-3

This edition first published in June 2002

Printed in the United States of America

Book design, Illustrations and cover by Derek Brigham
Website http//www.dbrigham.com
Tel/Fax: (612) 827-3431 • Email: dbrigham@visi.com
Photographs of the author by Don Pitlik: (612) 252-6797

DISCLAIMER
The author and publisher of this material are not responsible in any manner whatsoever for any injury
that may occur through following the instructions contained in this material. The activities, physical and
otherwise, described herein for informational purposes only, may be too strenuous or dangerous for
some people and the reader(s) should consult a physician before engaging in them.

Table of Contents

The development and maximization of speed...the new demands for explosive strength, agility, and power...the gridiron as modern battlefield... speed as the ultimate weapon for determining victory...how to annihilate the competition...what dictates success...how to produce a faster, more explosive athlete...the governing concept of effective training...the well-trained athlete's elixir to success.

The functional needs of the modern football player...how to maximize an individual's athletic development...the true and only goal of training...the Renegade Training success-mantra that every task must satisfy...the "no holds barred" and back-to-basics coaching philosophy for extreme physical prowess and the relentless pursuit of victory.

How I developed my blueprint for success...astonishing improvements in speed...the key determinant for successful conditioning...the vital importance of *periodization*...the real reason most athletes are not successful...formulating an appropriate plan of attack...regaining the work ethic for mental toughness and integrity...developing the pattern of victory as a daily mindset.

Flexibility as sport-specific range of motion...developing a functionally flexible athlete...the power of want and desire...the bending steel analogy...the three major effects of enhanced flexibility...extrafusal and intrafusal muscle fibers.

Static and dynamic flexibility...how to optimize static flexibility... training the cognitive process... how to optimize dynamic flexibility...understanding the vital difference between *stretching* and *range of motion development*.

ii   RENEGRADE TRAINING

Hip Mobility Exercises 3

1. Side Movement, Lead Leg Over (right leg from right side)
2. Side Movement Crossover Leg Over (right leg from left side)
3. Side Movement Alternate (from right side)
4. Front Movement From Side
5. Front Movement Down Center
6. Duck Under, Low Throughout
7. Duck Under, Pop Up Between
8. Duck Under, Twist, Low Throughout
9. Duck Under, Twist, Pop Up Between
10. Forward Zig-Zag, Duck Under

Tumbling Drills 21

How to use tumbling to improve body harmony and kinetic awareness...the many other benefits of tumbling drills.

1. Forward Roll to Stand
2. Backward Roll to Stand
3. Tripod to Stand

Postworkout Stretching 28

1. Side Right
2. Side Left
3. Crossover Right
4. Crossover Left
5. Middle Reach
6. Warrior Right
7. Warrior Left
8. Bent lunge Right
9. Bent lunge Left
10. Triangle Right
11. Triangle Left
12. Downward Dog
13. Cobra
14. Lower Back
15. Prayer Right
16. Prayer Left
17. Hurdle Right
18. Hurdle Left
19. Butterfly
20. Legs Apart Middle
21. Legs Apart Right
22. Legs Apart Left
23. Leg Under Right
24. Leg Under Left
25. Quad Right
26. Quad Left

Chapter 2—Agility Training   41

Why reaction, balance, and agility are better determinants of success on the football field than the 40-yard dash.

Rope Skipping   42

Rope skipping—the perfect exercise for everyone?...the nine skill areas addressed by rope skipping...the proper mechanics of rope work...selecting the best rope...the importance of correct hand position...rope speed.

Sequence Drills   44

1. Basic 2 feet together
2. Crossover of hands
3. Ali shuffle
4. Double-skips
5. Side-to-side slalom
6. Hip turns, feet parallel
7. Hip turns, left foot forward
8. Hip turns, right foot forward
9. High knees

Four rope routine patterns to employ during breaks, for greater physical benefits plus a heightened sense of awareness and concentration.

Agility Ladder   54

Ladder drills for foot positioning, quickness of feet, and efficiency of movement...how to make your own ladder.

Agility Ladder Drills   54

1. One foot per set of rungs
2. Two feet per set of rungs
3. Inside foot in and out, side-to-side fashion
4. Crossover foot in and out, side-to-side fashion
5. Lateral run
6. Lateral up-and-back run
7. Lateral shuffle
8. Lateral shuffle and turn
9. One-foot hop
10. Two-foot hop

Setting Up   85

Explosive Jump Training   88
Plyometric training to generate greater force and power...the importance of correct pre-conditioning...two drills for tremendous results.
  The Box Triple Jump
  Barrier Jumps

Power-Speed Skipping Drills   91
Brutal drills to enhance proper running form, develop the functional musculature of the midtorso, the proper pelvic tilt, and the hips, hamstrings, and lower levers needed for top speed.
  B Skips
  C Skips
  Butt Kicks
  High Knees

Chapter 4—Strength Development   95
How and why to avoid *muscular adaptation*...overcoming the adaptation curve—for tremendous gains in explosive power, speed, agility, and functional hypertrophy... improving motor skill ability...developing a lean, powerfully built football-perfect physique... the importance of creating deliberate chaos in your training.... addressing appropriate measures of absolute strength, speed strength, explosive strength, and strength endurance...starting strength ...acceleration strength...the *conjugate sequence* for strength training...*Special Physical Preparation*...the six key multiple-joint *focus lifts*.

Focus Lifts   96
  Clean and Power Clean
  Snatch and Power Snatch
  Dead Lifts
  Squats
  Push Press and Push Jerk
  Bench Press and Incline Press

Chart of Lifting Movements   97

Kettle Bell Lifts   98
Why kettlebell work should be an instrumental portion of any lifting program...kettlebells for muscular harmony, balance and powerful tendons...developing proper hip thrust for sport specific functions.

Foreword

As a football strength coach, I am constantly looking for ways to improve my team's athletic ability or—more importantly—speed.

Going into a game, I wanted to have the confidence that speed would not be a factor against us. I never wanted to walk off the field and say that we played good enough to win but we weren't good enough athletes or we weren't fast enough.

I didn't want to be the old-fashioned coach who says that we can only control the mental aspects of the game and not the physical. I wanted to have a program that would make a difference with my players. I wanted to have the physical advantage going into a game.

So, throughout my quest to achieve this goal, I have always been looking for programs that work. I've tried the "Add 50 pounds to your Bench Press" and "Drop .2 off your 40 in four weeks". We have run with parachutes as well as with other apparatus strapped to our bodies. In fact, I bought about every program I could find and talked to as many people as possible for ideas.

Some of the programs allowed for some success while others have been a failure.

The problem that I found with most programs was that they were nothing more than a collection of ideas or a theory without evidence. They never gave a true plan. The application of some of these ideas in a haphazard fashion could cause more harm than good; for example, performing plyometrics on a daily basis. Sure, an athlete could do the Sky King workout but the program never accounted for all the other aspects of training like flexibility or upper body strength.

So, my quest continued as I patched together programs and had moderate success, but not the success that I knew that I could achieve.

Finally, I read about John Davies in a Louie Simmons article. I called Louie and he gave me John's number. After a conversation with John, I purchased my first program. A couple of weeks later, John came to Chicago to make sure the program was being implemented properly. After four weeks I noticed a difference in my athletes.

It wasn't that the times were faster or anything I could prove with data but that the little things were noticeable. When they would run by, their foot strikes would sound faster. Most athletes were jumping and grabbing the rim. I could see a physical transformation in their posture and a decrease in body fat. It wasn't until the indoor track season that I could put some data together. By the end of the season, the track athletes that I had been working with had broken all of the school's sprint records.

The following fall their football team went 9-0, with three of the athletes going on to play Division 1 football. That spring, the same group reset the sprint records and placed in the state track meet in the top 5 in two events (actually one, we were disqualified for swearing).

Since then, we have had very successful football and track teams who use the Renegade Training program exclusively. The football team has a record of 24-6 in the last three years in a very competitive West Suburban Conference in the suburbs of Chicago. Our track teams are consistently one of the best in the state. I feel much of this success is due to the Renegade Training program.

There are many reasons why I think the Renegade Training has helped our program.

First, there is the simplicity of the program. There are no fancy uphill treadmills or multi-hip machines. Athletes don't strap themselves into strange contraptions held together with Velcro and Neoprene or walk around on some strange platforms glued to the bottom of their shoes. All you need to succeed in this program is dedication, perseverance, some flat ground and a good pair of shoes (also, don't eat right before you workout).

The Renegade program focuses on the basic fundamentals of movement. When these movements are drilled, they become second nature to the neural system, like a subconscious physical autopilot and consciously, the athlete can then focus on other aspects of competition, like winning. Athletes that have trained in this system stand out. Their lower bodies move with efficiency and quickness, as their heads stay focused on their keys. A coach can see the change during the workouts. Early in the program, athletes will not be able to talk or do much of anything else during their workouts. However, over time, they will learn to let their subconscious do the work and they will be able to talk, laugh and play games during their GPP and SPP sessions.

Second, the program's construction is a well-planned, traditional volume-building program. This allows athletes to systematically increase the amount of work their body can handle. Because the program is laid out over a period of time and suggests everything that should be done in each workout, overtraining and injuries no longer become a problem and progress is consistent. This is also helpful to the coach because he can plan for events and make sure his athletes are at their peak for the season or big meet. Too many times I have seen athletes that weren't physically prepared for the big meet because they have missed their peak.

Third and most importantly, the benefits of the program raise the entire level of the team. The poor become average, the average become good and the good become great. 5.81s become 5.31s, 5.21s become 4.91s. 4.71s become 4.51s. The program does not discriminate. Big, little, weak and strong, all those who go through the program will improve their athletic ability. If a team is "only as good as the weakest link", with the hard work and commitment that a team makes by starting this program then this program builds one strong chain.

I hope the Renegade program will do for you what it has done for my program: succeed.

Thanks
Chris Korfist
Track and Football Coach, Hinsdale Central High School, Illinois

The Renegade Creed

A choice for those without choices,
where victory is the only option.

The mission is simple: to seize the opportunity,
deny the competition, and establish dominance.

The work of Renegades is for neither the soft nor the weak.

Renegades are relentless in their attack
with a vicious and total commitment to their objectives.

Renegade Training breeds explosive, powerful, and fast athletes
who dictate the ebb and flow of competition
such that they are victorious.

If you are ready for the challenge—ready to master your athletic
destiny—then enter the world of Renegade Training.

Introduction

The game of football is firmly entrenched in the United States as a sporting pastime. It has evolved to become an extraordinary part of American culture, deeply woven into the fabric of the nation. For the many fans of the game, allegiance to a team is of utmost importance. They identify with their team, rejoicing in victory and suffering in defeat. While the notion may seem trite, for many, football is much more than a game. It's an experience that goes beyond simple sport. For those who have played the game, at any level, being a spectator brings back memories of teammates and camaraderie—learning how to work together for the common good.

On an individual level, the quest to be "the best" has driven many athletes, young and old, to strive for excellence and to stand among the finest. This pursuit has prompted the development of an endless array of approaches to physical preparation and ongoing debate over how to achieve intended goals. And with this fascination over athletics has come the philosophical argument of whether great athletes are born or made. Some believe that athletic ability is innate and lies hidden deep in the genetic code, much like an animal's bloodlines. Others contend that athletic excellence is produced by training and can be enhanced with a special elixir, nectar, or ambrosia, if you will. While it is true that an athlete's genetic traits cannot be altered, proper training and preparation can produce remarkable results. The development and maximization of speed, in particular, can be extraordinary.

The drive to be the best—among players as well as teams—has reached an unprecedented level, making year-round preparation paramount to success. Its difficult to pinpoint exactly when this occurred, but it was quite possibly within the legendary coaching career of Paul "Bear" Bryant that year-round training and preparation was first established. He was well known for his belief that victories are not made in the autumn but rather during the tough training months of the off season. To prepare adequately for the sport, no player, at any level, can enter training camp out of shape and expect to do well or secure a roster spot. Year-long preparation has been mandated as the standard of athleticism has constantly risen.

Thus, the demands of the playing football have changed dramatically as the game has evolved. The modern player is now an amazing balance of explosive strength, agility, and power. In fact, the gridiron is now akin to a modern battlefield, where the philosophies of conflict are apparent. Speed of movement has proven itself as the ultimate weapon throughout the history of conflict. Military strategists from the dawn of warring have recognized the invaluable role of speed in determining victory on the battlefield. Chinese military philosopher Sun Tsu, in his The Art of War, notes repeatedly that during a battle, speed will not only physically destroy the competition but also demoralize them emotionally.

Likewise, football has recognized the role of explosive power and speed as one of the most important (if not the most important) weapons in the athlete's arsenal. The notion that "Speed kills" has never been more evident than in today's game. An athlete who possesses explosive power and speed can use it to annihilate the competition. At every level of competition, speed and agility are heavily scrutinized and ultimately dictate success.

Clearly, when discussing speed and strength training for a football player, many things must be considered. Most important, to achieve the goal of producing a faster, more explosive athlete, all elements of training must support that intent. Paramount to success is the development of strength and mass such that it translates to improving sport-specific power and speed. The governing concept of effective training is simple: Develop explosive speed and power such that you can control the ebb and flow of the competition and therefore assist in achieving victory. Speed is the well-trained athlete's elixir for success.

Sadly, most training programs don't understand the functional needs of the modern football player. The level of confusion and misinformation about training is simply shocking. A review of the many training programs that have been published will make you wonder if these writers understand the needs of various sports or are merely trying to apply a uniform weight-lifting program to all sports, ignoring the all-important speed and agility components of football.

Regardless, we need to stop the debate about individual training approaches and focus on coaching an athlete for his or her function on the field. The division that has occurred among these various approaches has become the proverbial line drawn in the sand, as theorists argue the validity of their methodology over that of someone else. And so, while many point out how and why a given program will enhance strength development, they say little, if anything, about how it will affect performance on the field. Athletes are now often trained so that they achieve better results on testing day, even though what they have learned may not lead to better field performance.

It is a grievous mistake to coach athletes to test well and to post good numbers as opposed to training them to perform better on the field. The success of a training program should be determined by how much athletes improve their performance in competition, not by how well they perform a certain lift in a pristine testing environment.

The development of speed and power for playing football involves a complex balance of attributes, all of equal merit. Think of the construction of a great wheel, with each spoke representing a set of skills. For the wheel to move swiftly and powerfully, each spoke (or skill) must be carefully developed through receiving equal attention. To maximize an individual's athletic development, training must build a solid foundation of useable muscle, which is only as strong as its weakest link. Again, the goal of training should be to improve performance on the field, not only in the gym. Thus, the mantra for Renegade Training is form and function. Every task must satisfy this mantra.

To purists and historians, this approach will likely seem a throwback to a bygone era. Unequivocally, my work is different from the norm. Considered controversial by most coaches, even ruthless by some, it takes a "no holds barred" approach to assessing generally accepted training methods. But to achieve the success that my athletes have, we have had to break from the safe confines of the pack and think "outside the box." The concept behind my back-to-basics coaching philosophy is a return to a work ethic that builds athletes' physical prowess while encouraging their relentless pursuit of victory.

This philosophy wasn't borne of a hypothetical situation or clever marketing. It came from necessity. My own! As a young athlete, I dedicated myself voraciously to my own development. With some modesty, I can note that few have surpassed my dedication to training. In fact, I've been fortunate to have trained with some of the finest and most respected track and weight-lifting coaches known. But the results I achieved were never commensurate with the effort I put forth.

As time prevailed, I began to analyze this. I saw the errors of my own training repeated over and over by other athletes. Most important, their training didn't reflect the needs of their individual sports. Once I realized this, I began formulating the principles of Renegade training. And through exhaustive work over many years, I developed a blueprint for success.

Again, my own experience proved when I had found the right approach. At the age of 40, by applying the Renegade principles to my own training, I was able to sprint with many of the athletes I trained—even NFL wide receivers. I had become faster and more agile than when I was in my early twenties. My clients noted similar results. Damon Griffin, of the Cincinnati Bengals, has even noted that our work together saved his career. And within entire team environments, college- and pro-level players have seen such astonishing improvements in speed that they have been able to dictate the game plan and make up for many shortcomings of talent. Unequivocally, Renegade Training has become the solution to the needs of a modern football players.

We have all heard of spontaneous decisions and random actions that have proven fruitful in life. However, in conditioning for football, preparation is the key determinant to success. Within athletic development, the orderliness of training is called periodization. This concept is deeply entrenched in the Eastern bloc sports research community and is considered one of the factors that has brought these nations great success in the Olympics. Periodization is, by and large, the long-term organization of training as designed to maximize sport performance. The focus of a periodized plan of training is on preparing the athlete for the season ahead—and beyond, as well. The athlete's long-term success is primary, not just his or her immediate improvement.

Put simply, success is the offspring of hard work—brutally hard work—that follows a well-developed plan of attack. The reason that most athletes are not successful is that they have been victimized by poor long-term preparation. I get the most out of my athletes because in addition to making them work hard and want to win, my training involves careful planning. In the simplest terms, sports preparation requires a plan of attack that recognizes the specific needs of athletes on the football field. Performance is maximized through identifying the needs of the sport along with the individual athlete's weaknesses and then formulating an appropriate plan of attack.

The Renegade plan of attack incorporates these elements:

1. Range of motion development
2. Agility training
3. Linear speed development
4. Strength development
5. Work capacity development
6. Spiritual development

I will discuss each of these elements in detail in a chapter of this book. I will also evaluate the strengths and weaknesses of typical training programs and pass on my blueprint for success, Renegade style. In essence, to control the field of competition, we must master every discipline because, to quote Nietzsche, "No victor believes in chance."

The rewards of excellence on the field are quite diverse. Successful athletes learn the power of hard work and determination and the simple fact that anything worth having is worth working for. These rewards are earned at all levels of the sport. I have worked with some of the top teams and players in professional and collegiate football, yet I am particularly proud of the high school athletes I have coached who have applied the dedication of sport to areas of academic study. In fact, many young high school ball players have used the motivation of earning an athletic scholarship as a tangible reward for achievement on the field.

I would be remiss if I didn't note that regaining this work ethic is possibly one of the single-greatest benefits of the Renegade Training program. While I am proud to note the extraordinary testing-day accomplishments that my athletes have achieved, I am most proud of the mental toughness and integrity they have developed and the undeniable thirst for victory they have regained. These athletes have developed this pattern of victory during the hard training days of the off season and are known for their "never say die" attitude. For them and any athlete under my direction, success becomes established as a pattern of behavior.

Like nineteenth-century Prussian military leader Karl Von Clausewitz, athletes who believe in Renegade Training understand that "The human will is indefensible."

Chapter One

Range of Motion Development

Certainly, one of the most important, yet misunderstood, areas of athletic development is range of motion, or flexibility. It is often mistaken as simply stretching, more of a feminine skill or a passive activity, but it is neither. In fact, development in this area requires total dedication, an ability to work through the constant discomfort of improving range of motion. Several specific approaches to flexibility are detailed in the Renegade program, and I trust every Renegade will train in this area with a ferocious attitude.

I prefer to consider flexibility as sport-specific range of motion and not just a so-called stretching program. I put athletes through a group of different stretches that many consider more difficult than those done in their typical workouts, but that is only part of my total theory for developing a functionally flexible athlete. Other significant elements of Renegade Training are also effective in improving range of motion, such as hurdle/hip mobility work and weighted movements.

Every element of a player's development is affected by his or her functional flexibility. Whereas many athletes will have a difficult time attaining certain strength or speed goals, range of motion can be improved simply through want and desire. I suspect this idea comes from my history as a blacksmith and bending steel. If you heat an object and apply an easy, consistent tension, in time, the object will become pliable. Think of performing your flexibility program as a simple task like bending steel.

Enhanced flexibility has three major effects:

1. Muscular harmony and improved motor skills
2. Improved physical performance
3. Decreased muscular fatigue and injury

I should also note that improved range of motion results in an increase in the supply of blood and nutrients to joint structures. The level of synovial fluid, which lubricates the joints, also increases, further assisting in the transport of nutrients to the joints' articular cartilage.

A quick introduction to the basics of musculature might be warranted here. Muscles are composed of two types of fibers: extrafusal and intrafusal. Extrafusal fibers receive nerve impulses from the brain that cause the muscle fibers to shorten and contract. *Extrafusal fibers* contain *myofibrils*, small fibers that contract, relax, and elongate muscles. *Intrafusal fibers* serve the opposite function of extrafusal fibers. They are the main stretch receptors. When a muscle is stretched, the intrafusal fibers receive a message from the brain that initiates a stretch reflex. Thus, the movement of a muscle is controlled by the central nervous system. The speeds of nerve impulses are intensified with improved range of motion, thus increasing maximal speed of movement.

Static versus Dynamic Range of Motion

There are two types of range of motion or flexibility: static and dynamic. *Static* flexibility enhances the muscular range of motion and thus reduces the incidence of injury. It's achieved through the deep, tranquil relaxation of controlled muscular tension in a stretch position with complete control of breathing patterns. To reach this state, all tension must be eliminated from both the mental and physical aspects. Doing so is important in athletics because as an athlete begins to relax in competition, his or her actions involve less thought and more reflex. This so-called zone state is common to many great athletes. The mental aspect of sports will be discussed later in the book. For now, suffice it to say that to maximize training success, you must recognize and train the cognitive processes as well as the physical.

Dynamic flexibility is related more so to sport-specific movements. Extensive research has proven that enhancing dynamic range of motion directly improves performance. In fact, the greatest impact of flexibility training is manifested in performance characteristics. For that reason, enhanced range of motion is a central theme in Renegade Training. Each of our training programs offers an extensive array of both static and dynamic movements, such as hip/hurdle mobility training.

There is a great difference between the static and dynamic movements performed in hurdle mobility training. It's important to understand that *stretching* and *range of motion development* are not necessarily the same. Stretching, which is static, has many benefits in lengthening the muscle and reducing the incidence of injury. However, it will not necessarily impact sports performance. Developing the dynamic range of motion, on the other hand, is extraordinarily important. Again, numerous studies have proven that doing so contributes to greater athletic success in comparison to what can be achieved through improved static flexibility.

The preworkout stretching routine in the Renegade program is designed to work on the functional aspects of the sport and is more dynamic than static in nature. The exercises in this routine not only improve range of motion but also are great for football players, making them a perfect preamble to sport-specific work. A variety of 10 hip mobility exercises are performed with 5 hurdles of 2 to 5 sets. They are then followed with a series of tumbling movements and then a series of postworkout stretches.

Hip Mobility Exercises

1. **Side Movement, Lead Leg Over (right leg from right side)**

2. **Side Movement Crossover Leg Over (right leg from left side)**

3. **Side Movement Alternate (from right side)**

4. **Front Movement From Side**

5. **Front Movement Down Center**

6. **Duck Under, Low Throughout**

7. **Duck Under, Pop Up Between**

8. **Duck Under, Twist, Low Throughout**

9. **Duck Under, Twist, Pop Up Between**

10. **Forward Zig-Zag, Duck Under**

Note: The hurdles should be set at hip height for all 10 exercises.

1. Side Movement, Lead Leg Over
(right leg from right side):

Stand to the right side of the hurdles. Raise your lead leg over, maintaining a slight bend in the leg. Proceed to the next hurdle with a slight skip; be sure to stay on the balls of your feet as you plant each leg.

2. Side Movement Crossover Leg Over (right leg from left side)

Stand to the left side of the hurdles. Raise your crossover leg over, maintaining a slight bend in the leg. Again, proceed to the next hurdle with a slight skip, and stay on the balls of your feet as you plant each leg.

3. Side Movement Alternate (from right side)

Stand to the right side of hurdles. Raise your lead leg over (again, maintaining a slight bend) and then off to the side. Proceed to the next hurdle with a slight skip; stay on the balls of your feet.

4. Front Movement From Side

Stand facing the hurdles. Proceed with one leg at a time by raising each knee over the first hurdle. Proceed to the next hurdle with a slight skip; stay on the balls of your feet as you plant each leg.

5. Front Movement Down Center

Stand facing the hurdles. Raise your lead leg over the first hurdle, and then bring your trail leg over the second hurdle. (The hurdles must be set close enough to accommodate this.) Stay on the balls of your feet.

6. Duck Under, Low Throughout

Stand perpendicular to the hurdles. Duck under the first hurdle with your lead leg. Make sure your movement is initiated by pushing your buttocks back and that your feet always face forward. Stay in a low squat position throughout this drill.

Begin sliding underneath hurdle by pushing buttocks back and reaching forward with left leg.

Standing perpendicular to line with left hip facing hurdle.

Ensure feet are always pointed straight ahead.

Transfer weight from right to left side, and gather step right foot to left

Continue across as in other steps.

6B. Duck Under, Low Throughout with Kettlebell

A tremendous option for advanced development of the duck-under is to perform while holding a kettlebell.

7. Duck Under, Pop Up Between

Stand perpendicular to the hurdles. Duck under the first hurdle with your lead leg. Make sure your movement is initiated by pushing your buttocks back and that your feet always face forward. Pop up from the squatting position after you clear each hurdle.

Standing perpendicular to line with left hip facing hurdle.

Begin sliding underneath hurdle by pushing buttocks back and reaching forward with left leg.

As weight is transferred thrust hips forward and leap up.

Ensure feet are always pointed straight ahead.

Continue movement.

7B. Duck Under, Pop Up Between with Kettlebell

A tremendous option for advanced development of the duck-under, popup is to perform while holding a kettlebell.

8. Duck Under, Twist, Low Throughout

Stand perpendicular to the hurdles. Duck under the first hurdle with your lead leg, and then twist to lead under the second hurdle with your opposite leg. Make sure your movement is initiated by pushing your buttocks back and that your feet always face forward. Stay in a low squat position throughout the drill.

9. Duck Under, Twist, Pop Up Between

Stand perpendicular to the hurdles. Duck under the first hurdle with your lead leg, and then twist to lead under the second hurdle with your opposite leg. Make sure your movement is initiated by pushing your buttocks back and that your feet always face forward. Pop up from the squatting position after you clear each hurdle.

9B. Duck Under, Twist, Pop Up Between with Kettlebell

A tremendous option for advanced development of the duck-under, twist, popup is to perform while holding a kettlebell.

10. Forward Zig-Zag, Duck Under

Stand facing the hurdles, which are arranged in a zig-zag pattern, each successive hurdle offset one length from the previous hurdle. Duck under each hurdle, and pop up between them.

Tumbling Drills

Tumbling provides a tremendous form of drills to improve body harmony and kinetic awareness. Moreover, doing tumbling drills is a superb way to warm up for the rest of training. By using this series of simple drills, athletes will improve general balance and control:

1. **Forward Roll to Stand:** From a standing position, squat down and place both hands on the ground. Slowly roll forward and contact the ground with your head, tucking your chin to your chest and doing a somersault. Accelerate enough while doing the somersault so you have sufficient momentum to get on your feet and return to a standing position

2. **Backward Roll to Stand:** From a standing position, squat down and begin to roll backward. Place the palms of your hands on the ground behind your head, and as you begin to somersault backward, apply enough pressure to push off with your hands from the ground , get on your feet, and return to a standing position

3. **Tripod to Stand:** From a standing position, place both of your hands on the ground, shoulder-width apart. Squat down and form a tripod by bringing your knees up on your elbows. Roll forward slightly, curving your back and tipping your head to the ground. To move out of this position, gently roll your head back and up, straighten your back, and bring your legs down. As you roll out of the tripod, accelerate with your hips with enough momentum that you get on your feet and stand up.

1. Forward Roll to Stand

From a standing position, squat down and place both hands on the ground. Slowly roll forward and contact the ground with your head, tucking your chin to your chest and doing a somersault. Accelerate enough while doing the somersault so you have sufficient momentum to get on your feet and return to a standing position.

From standing position, walk towards spot where hands will be placed in beginning of somersault.

Place hands on floor and tuck chin into chest and slowly begin roll.

Continue to accelerate through forward somersault.

Accelerate hips
through to
contact.

As contact is
made leap
upwards.

2. Backward Roll to Stand

From a standing position, squat down and begin to roll backward. Place the palms of your hands on the ground behind your head, and as you begin to somersault backward, apply enough pressure to push off with your hands from the ground , get on your feet, and return to a standing position.

Standing upright with back to roll target.

Squat down with control.

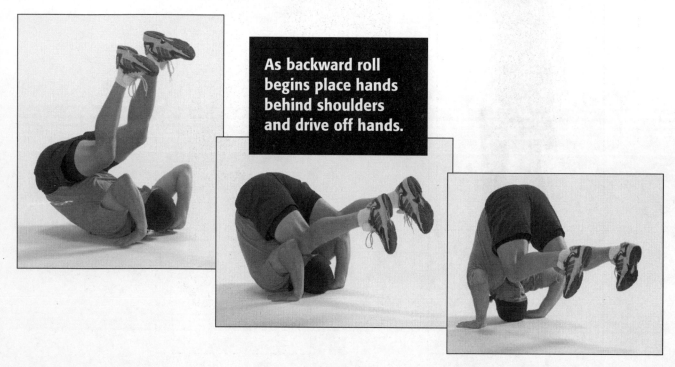

As backward roll begins place hands behind shoulders and drive off hands.

With push off from ground stand upright.

Continue with upwards leap.

3. Tripod to Stand

From a standing position, place both of your hands on the ground, shoulder-width apart. Squat down and form a tripod by bringing your knees up on your elbows. Roll forward slightly, curving your back and tipping your head to the ground. To move out of this position, gently roll your head back and up, straighten your back, and bring your legs down. As you roll out of the tripod, accelerate with your hips with enough momentum that you get on your feet and stand up.

Place hands on ground, shoulder-width apart with knees pressed firmly against elbows.

Place head on ground and slowly begin lifting on lower body upwards.

Continue lifting of lower body upwards.

Extend lower body up completely and hold.

Initiate rollout with tucking of chin and beginning to accelerate hips.

Make contact with ground.

Stand upright.

Postworkout Stretching

Postworkout stretching should be done to enhance recovery and should use the following stretches:

1. Side Right
2. Side Left
3. Crossover Right
4. Crossover Left
5. Middle Reach
6. Warrior Right
7. Warrior Left
8. Bent lunge Right
9. Bent lunge Left
10. Triangle Right
11. Triangle Left
12. Downward Dog
13. Cobra
14. Lower Back
15. Prayer Right
16. Prayer Left
17. Hurdle Right
18. Hurdle Left
19. Butterfly
20. Legs Apart Middle
21. Legs Apart Right
22. Legs Apart Left
23. Leg Under Right
24. Leg Under Left
25. Quad Right
26. Quad Left

1. Side right

Position legs spread wide apart and feet pointed straight ahead. Bend to right side, grasping ankle with right hand. Keep chest open towards front and bring left arm fully extended over left ankle.

2. Side left

Position legs spread wide apart and feet pointed straight ahead. Bend to left side, grasping ankle with left hand. Keep chest open towards front and bring right arm fully extended over left ankle.

3. Crossover right

Position legs spread wide apart and feet pointed straight ahead. Bend over and twist to right side, touching left foot with right hand. Twist torso and open chest to left side and look above, extending left arm straight above.

As left image but from side.

4. Crossover left

Position legs spread wide apart and feet pointed straight ahead. Bend over and twist to left side, touching right foot with left hand. Twist torso and open chest to right side and look above, extending right arm straight above.

5. Middle reach

Position legs spread wide apart and feet pointed straight ahead. Bend over from hips and grasp each ankle.

As left image but from side.

6. Warrior right (hands above)

Position legs spread wide apart, turn right foot out 90 degrees to right and left foot in. Twist body to right such that it faces direction of foot and outstretch hands as high as possible. Ensure knee of lead leg (right) does not extend past toe.

7. Warrior left

Optional stance of "warrior" stretch. Position legs spread wide apart, turn left foot out 90 degrees to left and right foot in. Reach out with left arm to left side and right arm back, such that arms are parallel to ground. Ensure knee of lead leg (right) does not extend past toe.

8. Bent lunge right

Position legs spread wide apart, turn right foot out 90 degrees to right and left foot in. Stretch down to right side and place right hand thru leg on ground to the right of the foot. Place left hand on ground directly across from right foot. Ensure back foot maintains full contact with ground.

9. Bent lunge left

Position legs spread wide apart, turn left foot out 90 degrees to left and right foot in. Stretch down to left side and place left hand thru leg on ground to the left of the foot. Place right hand on ground directly across from left foot. Ensure back foot maintains full contact with ground.

10. Triangle right

Position legs spread wide apart, turn right foot out 90 degrees to right and left foot in. Stretch down to right side and place right foot on top of ankle. Maintain chest open and facing forward, lift left arm straight up and look upwards.

11. Triangle left

Position legs spread wide apart, turn left foot out 90 degrees to left and right foot in. Stretch down to left side and place left foot on top of ankle. Maintain chest open and facing forward, lift right arm straight up and look upwards.

12 Downward Dog

With feet hip width apart
and knees slightly bent
place hands flat on ground
2-3 feet in front of you.
Straighten legs and look
upward to your navel.

13. Cobra

Pull hips through against ground and look upwards.

14. Lower Back

Ease back, pushing buttocks to heels and arms outstretched flat.

15. Prayer Right

Laying on ground, place right knee under chest and fold shin across. Keep back leg straight and reach arms outward with back as flat as possible.

Front angle of stretch.

16. Prayer Left

Laying on ground, place left knee under chest and fold shin across. Keep back leg straight and reach arms outward with back as flat as possible.

17. Hurdle Right

Outstretch right leg, with left foot against right thigh. Sit forward bending from the hip and grasp outside of right foot with right hand and inside of foot with left hand. Ensure shoulders are straight ahead and do not twist.

18. Hurdle Left

Outstretch left leg, with right foot against left thigh. Sit forward bending from the hip and grasp outside of left foot with left hand and inside of foot with right hand. Ensure shoulders are straight ahead and do not twist.

19. Butterfly

Bring feet in together at groin and gently push down with elbows.

20. Legs Apart Middle

Legs wide apart with toes pointed upward, ensuring feet don't roll outside. Sit forward by bending from the hip and grasp feet with respective hands.

21. Legs Apart Right

Legs wide apart with toes pointed upward, ensuring feet don't roll outside. Sit forward by bending from the hip and grasp right foot with right hand and left hand on inside of right ankle.

22. Legs Apart Left

Legs wide apart with toes pointed upward, ensuring feet don't roll outside. Sit forward by bending from the hip and grasp left foot with left hand and right hand on inside of left ankle.

23. Leg Under Right

With right leg extending and left knee against ground, ease back gently ensuring knee maintains or has near contact to ground.

With right leg extending and left knee against ground, ease back gently ensuring knee maintains or has near contact to ground. Repeat this ease back with left leg under stretch.

24. Leg Under Left

With left leg extending and right knee against ground, ease back gently ensuring knee maintains or has near contact to ground. Repeat easing back with left leg under stretch (as above).

25. Quad Right

From leg under position, situp and place right hand on ground. Pull left foot up towards buttocks and grasp foot with left hand.

26. Quad Left

From leg under position, situp and place left hand on ground. Pull right foot up towards buttocks and grasp foot with right hand.

Chapter Two

Agility Training

The media is responsible for the gross misrepresentation of sport speed that has prompted many young athletes and coaches to consider such tests as the 40-yard dash the sole determining factor in assessing an athlete's game-related speed. In fact, football is played within a smaller playing area, or "box," in which reaction, balance, and agility are the true determinants of success on the football field.

Agility training has tremendous merit in that it has an immediate and direct impact on athletic endeavors. Moreover, it lays the foundation for specialized physical preparation more than any other area of training. Therefore, it is a valuable element in the blueprint for Renegade Training.

Among my coaching peers, I am most well known for speed and agility training. I use a hybrid of training media:

1. Rope Skipping
2. Agility Ladders
3. Cone Drills
4. Bag Drills

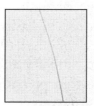   

Rope Skipping

The first phase of all agility training is rope skipping. Rope work is a centuries-old tradition and will certainly remain a steady component of all training in the future. It's relatively easy to learn, fully transportable, and inexpensive, and it offers extraordinary benefits to any level of player. It would be rare to find someone who wouldn't benefit from the use of rope work. Rope skipping might be the perfect exercise for everyone, from the youngest ball player to the advanced professional.

Bear in mind, the rope work involved in Renegade Training is not leisurely like the childhood game. I demand a torrid pace, as characterizes all the elements of the back-to-basics Renegade approach. Rope skipping at this demanding level will provide synergistic balance of numerous skill areas:

- Foot Speed
- Hand Speed
- Work Capacity
- Cardiovascular System
- Concentration
- Motor Skills/Body Harmony/timing
- Reduction of BodyFat
- Strengthening of Soft Tissue
- Balance

To start work, you must consider the proper mechanics of rope work. Luckily, the learning curve for rope work is very steep. Start your rope routine with moderation, and build up using a consistent and easy pace. While many training programs count jumps, I use time as the base. By employing various patterns of rope work, I am able to build up time in a similar geometric pattern as with the development of General Physical Preparation (GPP—see Chapter 5). Consider the first few weeks of rope training as a phase-in period. Your body will quickly adapt to the demands you make on it, and you will be able to attack this pursuit with *ferocity*.

In selecting a rope, choose one long enough so that when looped under your feet, it will reach chest height. There is no need to purchase an expensive rope; I prefer the inexpensive plastic models that can be easily adjusted.

The positioning of the hands on the rope can vary and will produce drastic differences. Most athletes allow their hands to drop naturally to their sides, so the speed of the rope relies mostly on wrist movement. This is a solid way to perform skipping.

However, an alternative style offers some interesting benefits for bicep development and increases the speed of the motion. Instead of allowing your hands to drop, pinch your elbows into your sides, such that your elbows to your wrist joints are roughly parallel to ground. This way, turning the rope involves the biceps and forearms in a major way. And once you adapt to this style, you will also notice a radical increase in the speed of the rope. Combative athletes, in particular, should use this style, as it's very applicable to the skills involved in throwing hooks/take downs and holds. The speed of the rope will vary significantly as you master this style; a speed in the range of 90 to 120 revolutions per minute is generally acceptable.

As you gain confidence in rope skipping, you will want to implement a pattern of movement in your rope work. You can perform a virtually endless array of work combinations, and you can always experiment. Even so, I use a simple pattern of rope movements throughout the total rope routine. As the athletes' work capacity improves, I direct them to perform 3-minute rounds with 1-minute active breaks, in which they execute a series of exercises.

If you maintain a steady regimen of rope work, you will be astonished at how quickly you advance. Once you are able to perform 3-minute rounds, you can also use the following sequence. The rope movement pattern that I prefer breaks the 3-minute rounds into 15-second splits. I suggest you use an alarm or a watch to signal moving from one pattern to the next. The constant changing provides a challenge and a nice degree of variation.

Here's the pattern of 15-second splits to be performed over 3 minutes:

Time (in seconds)	Sequence Drill
0–15	Basic 2 feet together
15–30	Crossover of Hands
30–45	Ali Shuffle
45–60	Double-Skips
60–75	Side-to-Side Slalom
75–90	Crossover of Hands
90–105	Hip Turns (feet parallel)
105–120	Crossover of Hands
120–135	Hip turns (left foot forward)
135–150	Crossover of Hands
150–165	Hip turns (right foot forward)
165–180	High Knees

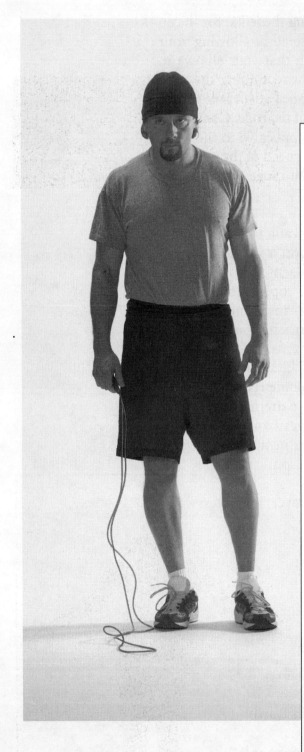

Descriptions of Sequence Drills

1. **Basic 2 Feet Together:** Jump with both feet together and only high enough to clear the rope passing underneath; speed is at the maximum pace.

2. **Crossover of Hands:** As the rope starts to pass overhead, quickly cross one hand over the other in a whipping fashion.

3. **Ali Shuffle:** Shuffle the feet back and forth in a manner like that of the legendary boxer.

4. **Double-Skips:** Jump high while turning the rope as fast as possible so that two revolutions of rope are completed for each single time the feet contact the ground.

5. **Side-to-Side Slalom:** With the feet together, jump quickly from side to side over an imaginary line. The distance of the jump should be small (roughly 6 inches) with minimal clearance as the rope passes underneath.

6. **Hip Turns (feet parallel):** Skipping with the feet together, quickly turn the hips back and forth, 90 degrees each turn.

7. **Hip Turns (left foot forward):** With the left foot in front, akin to a boxer's stance, quickly turn the hips from back to straight ahead to back to the starting stance.

8. **Hip Turns (right foot forward):** With the right foot in front, akin to a boxer's stance, quickly turn the hips from back to straight ahead to back to the starting stance.

9. **High Knees:** Run in place with the knees high.

1. Basic 2 Feet Together

Basic 2 foot ground contact.
Ensure hands are above hips.

2. Crossover of Hands
As rope begins to clear above head, quickly cross-over hands in a whipping fashion and back.

3. Ali Shuffle

Shuffle feet back and forth with approximately a 1-2 foot spacing.

4. Double-Skips

As rope begins to clear feet, explode upward while increasing .speed of rope, such that 2 revolutions occur.

5. Side-to-Side Slalom
With feet together hop side to side.

6. Hip Turns (feet parallel)
Twist torso and legs keeping feet pallel.

7. Hip Turns (left foot forward)

Twist torso and legs so that left foot comes forward and has turned 90 degrees.

8. Hip Turns (right foot forward)

Twist torso and legs so that right foot comes forward and has turned 90 degrees.

9. High Knees
Run with knees at hip height.

Next, let me explain the exercise patterns that are employed during the breaks. Beyond the various physical benefits of using this circuit method, many athletes also notice a heightened sense of awareness or concentration that they can quickly adapt for their work on the gridiron. These exercises also coincide with additional work performed in the day, and a sampling of them follows.

Given that each full round is 4 minutes (3-minute rope sequence + 1-minute break), it's easy to calculate the time you can afford to spend, whether you are working out for personal conditioning or for more a sport-specific purpose. For most purposes, I use 6-round sessions (24 minutes total) employing these four rope routines:

Descriptions of Rope Routines

Rope Routine A: To coincide with pushing day movements
Rounds 1, 2, and 3   30 seconds of fisted pushups
Rounds 4, 5, and 6   30 seconds of dips

Rope Routine B: To coincide with pulling day movements
Rounds 1, 2, and 3   30 seconds of burpees
Rounds 4, 5, and 6   30 seconds of towel chins

Rope Routine C: For active recovery
Rounds 1, 2, and 3   30 seconds of vertical hops (quick pace)
Rounds 4, 5, and 6   30 seconds of slalom hops (quick pace)

Rope Routine D: Functional hybrid (increase break to 90 seconds)
Rounds 1, 3, and 5   30 seconds of pushups (not to failure!)
                            + 15 burpees
Rounds 2, 4, and 6   30 seconds of towel chins (not to failure!)
                            + 15 burpees

Agility Ladder

The second element in Renegade agility training is the agility ladder. Athletes run through the ladder with their heads up, as if on a swivel, so they can see everything around them. Ladder drills teach a tremendous variety of skills, included foot positioning, quickness of feet, and efficiency of movement. Ladder work should be performed in the most sport-specific manner possible.

Ladders can be bought ready made or constructed of simple 18-inch squares. In my training, I create the ladder with rope or with taped lines laid out evenly, 18 inches apart, over an 8-yard distance.

The following agility ladder drills should be performed on a regular basis. Each drill should be done twice with minimal rest between sets (say, 30 seconds). The diagrams provided show the direction and placement of each foot. Foot patterning is termed "R" or "L" for "Right" and "Left," and the numbers refer to sequencing. The starting points of the feet are not numbered. Because some of the movements occur outside the ladder, I have shadowed the actual ladder.

Agility Ladder Drills

1. One Foot per set of Rungs

2. Two Feet per set of Rungs

3. Inside Foot In and Out, Side-to-Side Fashion

4. Crossover Foot In and Out, Side-to-Side Fashion

5. Lateral Run

6. Lateral Up-and-Back Run

7. Lateral Shuffle

8. Lateral Shuffle and Turn

9. One-Foot Hop

10. Two-Foot Hop

1. One Foot per set of Rungs:

Run such that you place one foot between each successive set of rungs. (That is, step between the rungs.)

Knees up with strong contact to surface and powerful arm thrust.

Ensure athlete's butt is back with eyes up and aware of actions in front of them.

Renegade Training™
Copyright ©2002
John K. Davies
Dragon Door Publications, Inc.
1-800-899-5111
www.dragondoor.com

2. Two Feet per set of Rungs:

Run such that you place two feet between each successive set of rungs.

Same fundamentals as with one foot per rung drill but ensure both feet make contact in each rung.

Renegade Training™
Copyright ©2002
John K. Davies
Dragon Door Publications, Inc.
1-800-899-5111
www.dragondoor.com

3. Inside Foot In and Out, Side-to-Side Fashion

Run in a side-to-side fashion, starting to the side of the ladder. Place your inside (lead) foot between the first set of rungs, and then place your outside (back) foot between the same set of rungs. Next, step with your lead foot outside the ladder, followed by your back foot. As your back foot comes down outside the ladder, it becomes your lead foot, and the same sequence of movements is repeated.

Starting to left of ladder with athlete low.

Initiate first movement with hard plant into first rung with right foot.

Continued next page.

Renegade Training™
Copyright ©2002
John K. Davies
Dragon Door Publications, Inc.
1-800-899-5111
www.dragondoor.com

Left foot trails into rung.

Right foot comes out and plants.

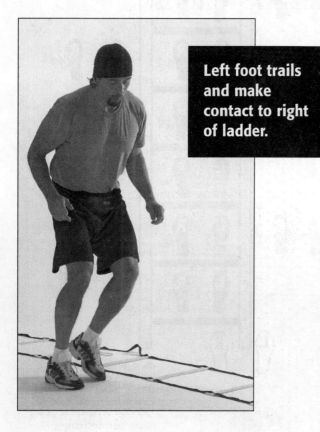

Left foot trails and make contact to right of ladder.

As left foot makes contact to right of ladder immediately pickup and cutback hard to inside of rung with same foot.

4. Crossover Foot In and Out, Side-to-Side Fashion

Run in a side-to-side fashion, starting to the side of the ladder. Place your outside (lead) foot between the first set of rungs by stepping across your inside foot; then step with your inside (back) foot behind your lead foot to place it between the same set of rungs. Next, step with your lead foot outside the ladder, followed by your back foot. As your back foot comes down outside the ladder, it becomes your lead foot, and the same sequence of movements is repeated.

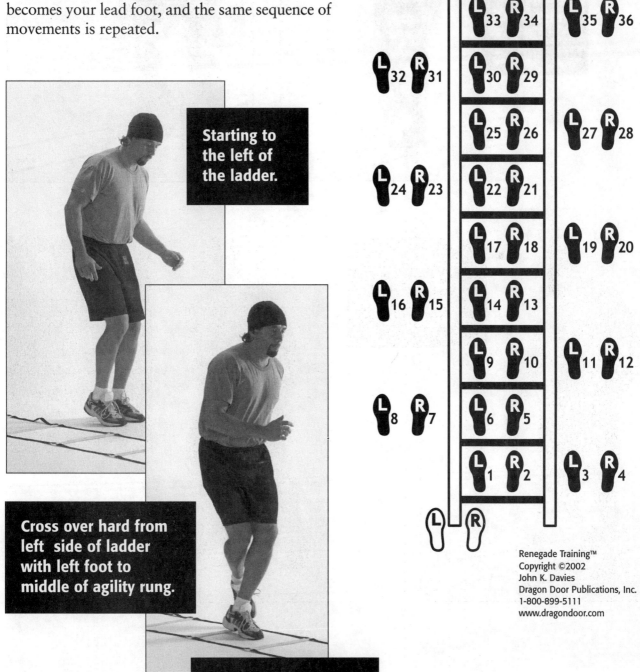

Starting to the left of the ladder.

Cross over hard from left side of ladder with left foot to middle of agility rung.

Continued next page.

Renegade Training™
Copyright ©2002
John K. Davies
Dragon Door Publications, Inc.
1-800-899-5111
www.dragondoor.com

Cross over hard from right side of ladder with right foot to middle of rung.

5. Lateral Run

Perform this drill in a sideways position to the ladder. Sit back on your hips, buttocks out, emulating a two-point positional stance. Move to the side, placing both feet between each successive set of rungs.

Run laterally with high knees making strong ground contact and vigorous arm power.

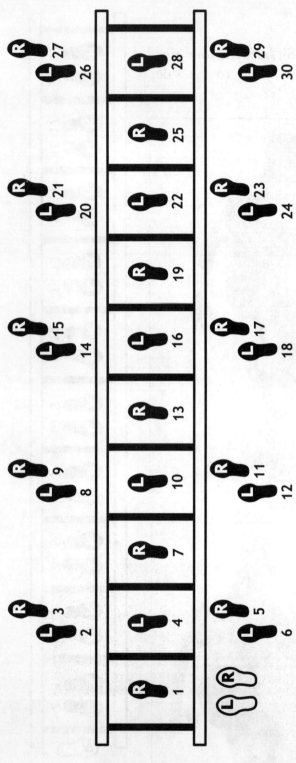

Renegade Training™
Copyright ©2002
John K. Davies
Dragon Door Publications, Inc.
1-800-899-5111
www.dragondoor.com

6. Lateral Up-and-Back Run

Perform this drill in a sideways position to the ladder. Sit back on your hips, buttocks out, emulating a two-point positional stance. Start at the top of the ladder. Moving to your left, perform this series of steps: Attack forward by placing your right foot between the first set of rungs and then your left foot between the next set of rungs. Next, move your right foot back, stepping between the previous set of rungs. Attack forward again, starting once more with your right foot, and stay low in a two-point positional manner.

Standing below ladder, attack with lead foot into rung.

Run through ladder with offside foot above ladder. Ensure hips are low as athlete attacks across the ladder.

Drive lead foot above top of ladder.

Upon contact of lead leg, immediately dig off-side foot back to middle of rung.

7. Lateral Shuffle

Perform this drill in a sideways position to the ladder. Sit back on your hips, buttocks out. Moving to your left, perform this series of steps: Place your left foot between the first set of rungs, and then place your right foot in the next set of rungs. Repeat the same two steps but beginning with the opposite foot each time. Keep your feet and hips pointed straight ahead. Shuffle on the balls of your feet, and perform quick movements that are initiated from your hips.

Start with lead foot in rung, off-side foot behind ladder.

Pivot from hips and alternate moving down ladder with shuffle of hips.

Renegade Training™
Copyright ©2002
John K. Davies
Dragon Door Publications, Inc.
1-800-899-5111
www.dragondoor.com

8. Lateral Shuffle and Turn

Perform this drill in a sideways position to the ladder. Sit back on your hips, buttocks out. Moving to your left, perform this series of steps: Place your left foot between the first set of rungs, and then place your right foot in the next set of rungs. Repeat the same two steps but beginning with the opposite foot each time. To do so, turn your hips/torso such that your right foot and body not completely face left far side of ladder. With the next motion, turn your body back straight ahead. Keep your feet and hips pointed straight ahead. Shuffle on the balls of your feet, moving across the rungs, and perform quick movements that are initiated from the hips.

Start with lead foot in rung, off-side foot behind ladder.

Pivot from hips and thrust torso around so that athlete is facing directly ladder. As athlete turns, quickly lift hands up as if to catch ball.

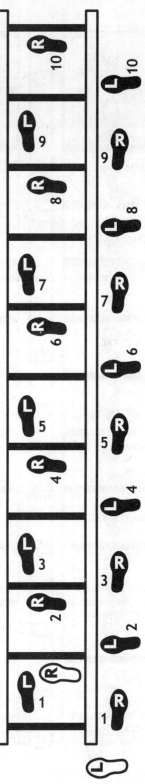

Renegade Training™
Copyright ©2002
John K. Davies
Dragon Door Publications, Inc.
1-800-899-5111
www.dragondoor.com

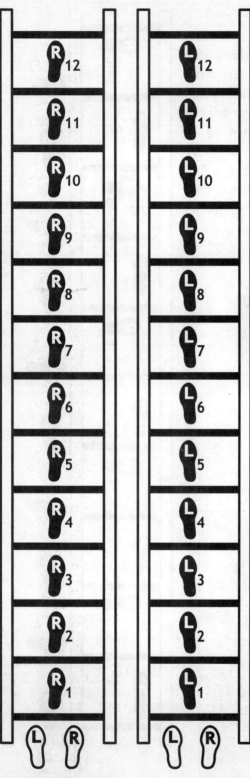

9. One-Foot Hop

Hop forward on one foot between successive sets of rungs, making solid contact on the ball of your foot. Repeat with opposite foot.

Hop quickly on one foot.

67

10. Two-Foot Hop

Hop forward on both feet between successive sets of rungs, making solid contact on the balls of your feet.

Hop quickly on one foot.

Renegade Training™
Copyright ©2002
John K. Davies
Dragon Door Publications, Inc.
1-800-899-5111
www.dragondoor.com

Bag Drills

Another basic element in Renegade agility training is bag drills. Bag drills closely mimic actual playing conditions and are typically done only during the final 6-week phase of training that focuses on specialized physical preparation. Bag drills should be performed with tackling dummies. Use five bags and arrange them approximately 3 feet apart. Set up each bag using a 3-yard box above and below the bag to simulate sport-specific game conditions.

Perform each of the following drills on a regular basis, twice to a side:

1. Forward Run Over Bags

2. Forward Run/Chop Over Bag

3. Forward Zig-Zag Around Bags

4. Forward Shuffle Around Bags

5. Lateral Run Over Bags

6. Lateral Run Down and Attack Around Bags

1. Forward Run Over Bags

Run forward over each bag, one foot hitting the ground between each successive pair of bags (i.e., alternating feet).

Run forward with one foot contact between each bag.

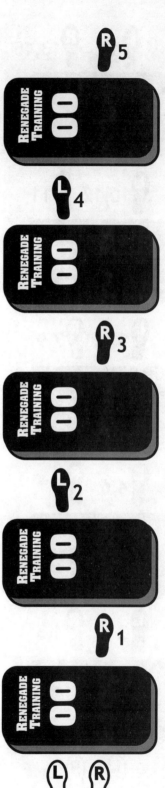

Renegade Training™
Copyright ©2002
John K. Davies
Dragon Door Publications, Inc.
1-800-899-5111
www.dragondoor.com

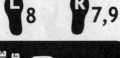

2. Forward Run/Chop Over Bag

Run forward over each bag, making three foot contacts between each pair of bags (i.e., three steps: lead, trail and lead "chop").

Run forward with three hard foot contacts between each bag.

Renegade Training™
Copyright ©2002
John K. Davies
Dragon Door Publications, Inc.
1-800-899-5111
www.dragondoor.com

3. Forward Zig-Zag Around Bags

Run forward and around bag obstacles, planting the foot on the outside cut. Stay low through the cuts.

Accelerate into cut.

Plant hard and accelerate up bag.

Renegade Training™
Copyright ©2002
John K. Davies
Dragon Door Publications, Inc.
1-800-899-5111
www.dragondoor.com

4. Forward Shuffle Around Bags

Run forward and around bag obstacles by sliding laterally, down/up, and then forward again.

Shuffle across, hands outstretched & head up

Renegade Training™
Copyright ©2002
John K. Davies
Dragon Door Publications, Inc.
1-800-899-5111
www.dragondoor.com

5. Lateral Run Over Bags

Perform a lateral run over each bag, making two foot contacts between each successive pair of bags (i.e., two steps).

High knee, eyes up and head on a swivel to be aware of all movement.

Renegade Training™
Copyright ©2002
John K. Davies
Dragon Door Publications, Inc.
1-800-899-5111
www.dragondoor.com

6. Lateral Run Down and Attack Around Bags

Starting perpendicular to the first bag, run forward just enough to clear the bag, lateral across the bag, quickly backpeddle between the first and second bags, and then lateral across the second bag. Repeat this series of steps so as to go around all the bags. Circumvent bag obstacles and maintain a two-point positional stance.

Eyes up and head on a swivel to be aware of all movement.

Cone Drills

Cone drills—the final element in agility training—are performed throughout Renegade Training but at different levels of intensity, depending on the training cycle. For the first three cycles of the off season, athletes should perform at 75% of their maximal output with 30 to 45 seconds of rest between sets. In the final cycle, athletes should perform at 100%.

This type of drill uses regular traffic-type cones set up in specific patterns. They are set 5 to 10 yards apart so as to mimic the true aspect in football of "playing in a box." The focus in these drills is acceleration. For each of the following series, each pattern should be run twice using the movement described. Start each from a two-point positional stance, similar to that of game condition. And come in and out of the cuts as low as possible.

Series 1—Box

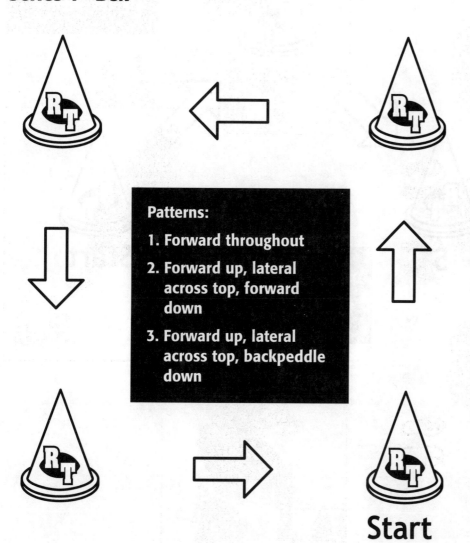

Patterns:

1. Forward throughout

2. Forward up, lateral across top, forward down

3. Forward up, lateral across top, backpeddle down

Start

Renegade Training™
Copyright ©2002
John K. Davies
Dragon Door Publications, Inc.
1-800-899-5111
www.dragondoor.com

Series 1–"X"

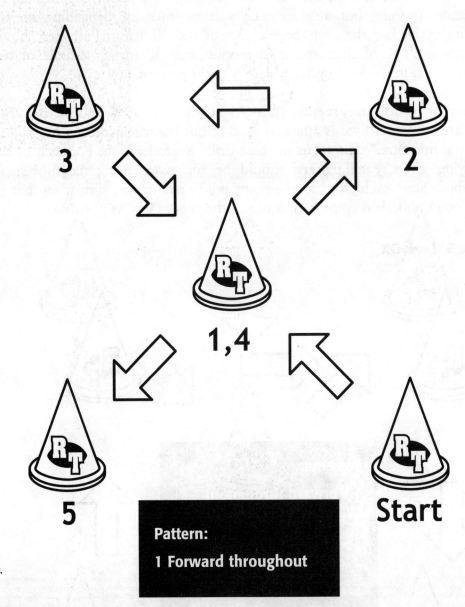

3

2

1,4

5

Start

Pattern:

1 Forward throughout

Series 1—Star

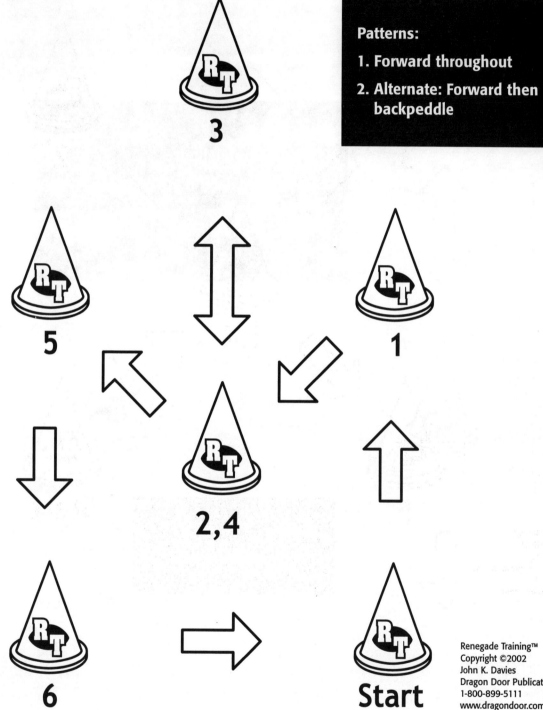

Patterns:

1. Forward throughout
2. Alternate: Forward then backpeddle

3

5

1

2,4

6

Start

Renegade Training™
Copyright ©2002
John K. Davies
Dragon Door Publications, Inc.
1-800-899-5111
www.dragondoor.com

Series 2—Chair

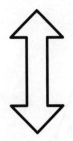

Patterns:

1. **Forward throughout**

2 **Forward up, lateral across top, forward down**

3. **Forward, lateral, forward, backpeddle down**

Renegade Training™
Copyright ©2002
John K. Davies
Dragon Door Publications, Inc.
1-800-899-5111
www.dragondoor.com

Start

Series 2—"M"

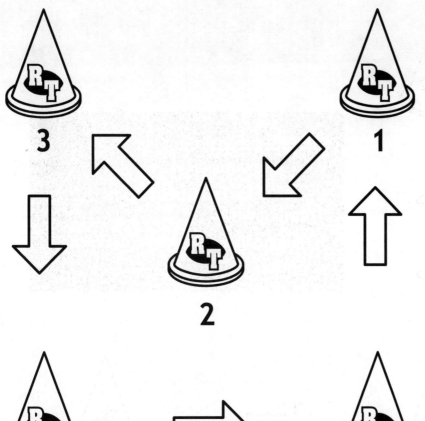

3

1

2

4

Start

Renegade Training™
Copyright ©2002
John K. Davies
Dragon Door Publications, Inc.
1-800-899-5111
www.dragondoor.com

Patterns:

1. **Forward throughout**

2. **Alternate: Forward then backpeddle**

Chapter Three

Linear Speed Development

My thoughts on the significance of speed can be summed up in this quote from *The Art of War,* by Sun Tzu: "Speed is the essence of war." As noted earlier, I am known in training circles for my focus on and success in improving athletes' game speed.

Improving absolute speed is, in fact, a by-product of developing the skills explained in the other chapters: range of motion, agility, strength, and work capacity. The model of improving game speed is simply a balanced training approach, as discussed in the Introduction as the Renegade plan of attack. By following this plan, you will be able to develop the necessary tools to enhance your game speed. Special sprint training will employ a variety of drills to maximize absolute speed.

In the simplest of terms, an athlete's top speed is his or her Rate of Stride x Stride Length. However, that top speed can only be achieved with the precise proportion of each factor: rate and length. Given this, proper form is essential. Developing the proper form through physical development will quickly enhance speed.

Unfortunately, many athletes do not have good form. For example, many lack the torso stability to maximize their speed. This problem can be easily solved by strengthening the abdominal wall and spinal erectors. The driving, pumping action of the arms is also crucial to speed development. The shoulder girdle (as well as the hands) needs to relax as the motion is generated from it with arm angle of approximately 90 degrees.

Sprint Sequences

Sprinting is made up of three basic phases:

1. **Drive,** with power coming off the balls of the feet conveying lower lever strength
2. **Recovery,** with the foot clearing the ground as the thigh swings forward from the hip
3. **Support,** with total foot contact

To maximize improvement in sprinting, work should be broken into maximal work and submaximal work. *Maximal work* is fairly straightforward, comprising sprints that begin from a three-point start (mixed on your own decision or cadence), a two-point positional start, and a flying 10-yard start (i.e., a running start, which is done by starting with a jog 10 yards before the start line and gradually accelerating to full speed at the start line). Maximal work should be performed at 100% effort; a minimum of 72 hours should be allowed for recovery between sessions. *Submaximal work*, on the other hand, is less intense. It should be performed at 60% to 75% of maximal output.

The Renegade Training approach follows several easy patterns, which can be combined in a weekly program. Maximal work should be performed on pulling/squat days, and submaximal work should be performed on pushing/bench press days. Changing sprint distances also offers considerable variation in training.

Note: In the following sequences, a notation such as "75 x 2" means "perform two 75-yard sprints."

Maximal Work

Sequence A
> 75 x 2, from flying 10-yard start
> 50 x 2, from three-point start
> 65 x 2, from two-point positional start
> 20 x 2, from three-point start on cadence

Sequence B
> 55 x 2, from flying 10-yard start
> 25 x 3, from three-point start
> 40 x 2, from two-point positional start
> 10 x 3, from three-point start on cadence

Sequence B: Sled Option (performed with running sled, lightly loaded)

45 x 2, from flying 10-yard start

15 x 2, from three-point start on cadence

25 x 2, from two-point positional start

10 x 2, from three-point start on cadence

Submaximal Work

Renegade Gassers

These grueling exercises are generally performed twice a week to improve acceleration. They are made up of four stages of sprints. In stage 1, the athlete accelerates to 75% of his or her top speed by the 15-yard mark, maintains that speed until the 40-yard mark, and then slowly decelerates. At the 55-yard mark, the athlete makes a wide, 10-yard semicircle and returns to the starting line for stage 2, which is the return to stage 1. Stages 3 and 4 are identical to 1 and 2, respectively.

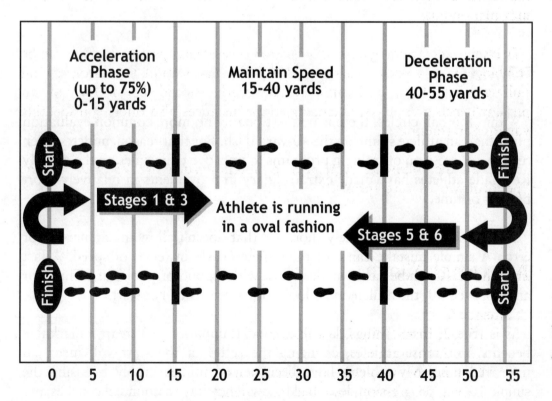

Renegade Training™
Copyright ©2002
John K. Davies
Dragon Door Publications, Inc.
1-800-899-5111
www.dragondoor.com

Circuit Runs

Each of the following circuits contains five sets of runs, which should be performed in order with the rest times indicated. The athlete should perform at 70% of capacity, and he or she should concentrate on proper form.

Circuit A
1. 100, 100, 100: 20-yard walks between intervals; rest 90 seconds
2. 100, 100 x 2, 100: 20-yard walks between intervals; rest 90 seconds
3. 100 x 2, 100, 100 x 2: 20-yard walks between intervals; rest 90 seconds
4. 100, 100 x 2, 100: 20-yard walks between intervals; rest 90 seconds
5. 100, 100, 100: 20-yard walks between intervals

Circuit B
1. 75, 75, 75: 20-yard walks between intervals; rest 90 seconds
2. 75, 75 x 2, 75: 20-yard walks between intervals; rest 90 seconds
3. 75 x 2, 75, 75 x 2: 20-yard walks between intervals; rest 90 seconds
4. 75, 75 x 2, 75: 20-yard walks between intervals; rest 90 seconds
5. 75, 75, 75: 20-yard walks between intervals

The 40

Within football circles, there is unquestionably no more common evaluation point than an athlete's time on the 40-yard dash. For that reason, athletes often turn to a succession of training programs to improve their times on the 40. My Renegade athletes have made extraordinary improvements in relatively short periods of time.

In fact, the 40 is an extremely short test that doesn't allow much margin for error. A simple mistake can cost the athlete dearly in terms of speed. A fast time on the 40 can be easily made or lost with a good or poor start. Thus, for an improved 40, the athlete must look to master his or her start.

As is true of many things, laying a good foundation will reap remarkable benefits. For most athletes, changing the setup of the start will mean an improved time. My athletes have been helped immeasurably by using the simple 10-step progression described below. They have astounded coaches and scouts with their quick improvements in running the 40.

Setting Up

1. Step up to the start line, aligning the toes of both feet on the edge of the line.
2. Most athletes prefer to place their left foot in front of them for both comfort and power.
3. Place your left foot a few inches directly behind your right foot. The front of your left foot will be approximately 16 inches behind the start line.
4. Kneel down, placing your right knee directly next to the ball of your left foot. Keep your right knee and your left foot roughly 6 to 8 inches apart.
5. Place your right hand on the start line, spreading your fingers wide and arching your palm so as to keep it off the ground. Keep your left arm back.
6. Your weight should be balanced with the majority being supported by your legs but some being supported by your lead foot. Ensure that you can apply enough pressure in starting.
7. Your left leg should be bent at a 90-degree angle.
8. Your right leg should be bent at a 135-degree angle.
9. Your left arm should be bent at roughly a 135-degree angle, with your elbow above your torso but your hand slightly higher than your hip joint.
10. Relax your body and visualize a successful start, followed by executing all facets of the race properly.

Step up to the start line, aligning the toes of both feet on the edge of the line.

Place your left foot a few inches directly behind your right foot. The front of your left foot will be approximately 16 inches behind the start line.

Kneel down, placing your right knee directly next to the ball of your left foot. Keep your right knee and your left foot roughly 6 to 8 inches apart.

Place your right hand on the start line, spreading your fingers wide and arching your palm so as to keep it off the ground. Keep your left arm back.

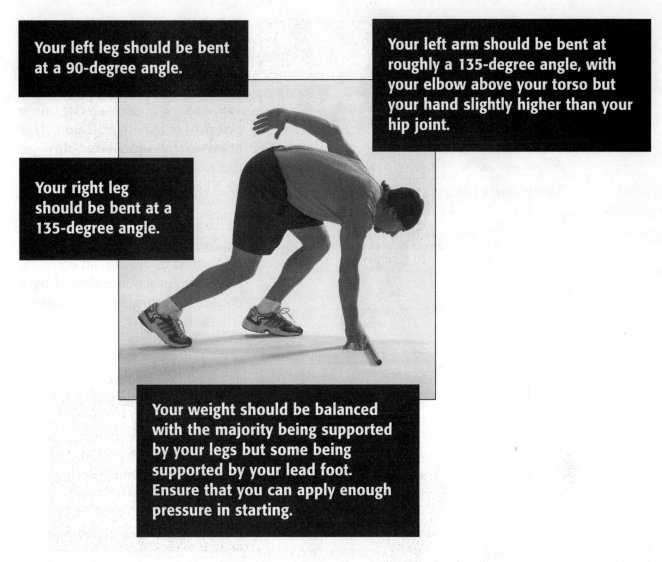

Your left leg should be bent at a 90-degree angle.

Your left arm should be bent at roughly a 135-degree angle, with your elbow above your torso but your hand slightly higher than your hip joint.

Your right leg should be bent at a 135-degree angle.

Your weight should be balanced with the majority being supported by your legs but some being supported by your lead foot. Ensure that you can apply enough pressure in starting.

Practice this setup enough so it becomes second nature to you.

To run the 40, the athlete should accelerate steadily from the initial drive off the line through to the finish. In driving off the line, the athlete should be low and have a feeling of pushing backward and down to start the sprint while simultaneously controlling the "rip" of the right arm and the "hammering" back of the left.

Training in the 40 should also focus on the need for the athlete to relax throughout running the race. This relaxed state can only be accomplished by an athlete who has mastered all of the elements of conditioning. Confidence comes from knowing that he or she has the ability to run a good race. I have heard many professional scouts say that a quality time on the 40 signals an athlete who has dedicated himself or herself to the sport and leaves nothing to chance.

Explosive Jump Training

Plyometric training was first used in the United States after "emigrating" from European coaches, who described it as a supposedly secret training protocol of the Soviet Union. This approach was pioneered through the work of Soviet coach Yuri V. Verkhoshansky.

Plyometric drills (often called explosive jump or shock drills) are performed to develop an eccentric muscle contraction followed by a concentric muscle contraction, which is known as the stretch-shortening cycle. This type of training can help an athlete generate greater force and power. However, it is imperative that this work be done only after significant conditioning bases have been achieved. Most conditioning programs jump (pardon the pun) into plyometric training without having developed this level of conditioning.

Renegade Training builds up to this type of training in a controlled manner, such that the athlete can achieve maximum results. While many different drills (and media) can be used for this type of training, I find these two drills bring tremendous results with movements of the lower extremities.

Box Triple Jump

Begin standing on a short box. Walk off the box slowly, and plant your left foot flat on the ground. Then make a quick impulse jump forward with your right leg, driving your knee up and out. As your right foot lands on the ground, drive your left knee up and out. Then make another quick impulse jump with your right leg.

Standing on low box.

Walk off with left foot softly.

Explode upwards with left knee up and out.

Barrier Jumps

Place five hurdles roughly three feet apart each. Set the height even with the hip joint. Relax and leap over the first barrier. After you land, quickly leap over the next in an explosive movement. Perform this exercise with an element of flow. Allow your body to learn how to perform a difficult move in an easy manner.

Standing in front of barrier, roughly set at hip height explode upward.

Drive knees up to chest.

As you make contact, immediately explode upwards to next barrier.

Power/Speed Skipping Drills

Power/speed skipping drills are a brutal component of Renegade Training—often, the most grueling element of any training session. They are performed not only to enhance proper running form but also to develop the functional musculature of the midtorso, the proper pelvic tilt, and the hips, hamstrings, and lower levers needed for top speed. Many athletes have developed strong abdominals but don't perform the correct motor patterns while moving at top speed.

B Skips

Skip with your lead knee coming up and down with some force but at an easy cadence. Alternate skipping motion between legs. Also ensure the proper thrusting arm movement.

C Skips

Skip with your lead knee coming up, and then extend your foot out. Sweep your foot down with force, propelling your body forward. As in a B skip, alternate between right and left leg strikes.

Butt Kicks

While doing a slow jog, vigorously kick your heels to your buttocks. Your hip-to-knee joints should remain relatively still. All the action should come from your knee-to-foot lever.

High Knees

This drill involves a progression of B skips and is possibly the most demanding leg exercise done in the program. Life your knees to your hip joints, and then drive them down in a fast and constant pace.

Chapter Four

Strength Development

Many of the basic principles of Renegade Training are completely inherent to the task at hand and the function of performance on the field. Our long-term training plan recognizes the value of consistently varying exercise stimuli so as to avoid muscular adaptation.

Over time, the body will adapt to a given training regimen, and results will lag according to a sort of law of diminishing returns. Once they overcome the adaptation curve, athletes make tremendous gains in terms of explosive power, speed, agility, and functional hypertrophy. In addition, they are able to maintain a sense of training enthusiasm because of the refreshing stimuli and new challenges. The wide variety of exercise in the Renegade program also leads to improved motor skill ability, which translates into sport-specific skills on the gridiron. Athletes unilaterally tend to develop a lean but powerfully built physique, perfectly suited for the purposes of playing football.

Another benefit that comes from the relentless and diverse nature of Renegade Training is the creation of an element of *chaos*, which proves to be invaluable in the heat of battle. The successful warrior or athlete must be comfortable in the chaos of competition. And that comfort is developed through effective training. Being determined, having the will and stamina to succeed against adversity, and possessing a wide repertoire of physical skills— all of these principles become part of the underlying philosophy of teams and athletes who follow the Renegade Training approach.

Within the context of strength characteristics, I maintain that all training must address appropriate measures of absolute strength, speed strength, explosive strength, and strength endurance. Within the parameters of the gridiron, absolute strength, starting strength, and acceleration strength are clearly paramount to the athlete's success. As defined by Dr. Mel C. Siff, in *Supertraining 2000*, "Starting strength is the ability to quickly develop the greatest possible force at the initial moment of tension" and "Acceleration strength is the ability to build up working force as rapidly as possible once contraction has occurred." In developing speed strength, the focus must be on generating bar speed and producing a dynamic force. The speed of the bar is key here. It's not simply the weight that's being moved but the speed at which that's happening. Newton's second law states that force is determined by considering mass and velocity.

Within strength-training programs, a system known as the conjugate sequence is employed. It uses different training phases in which responses are elicited for enhancing the ultimate *SPP*, or *Special Physical Preparation*.

The Renegade strength development program uses multiple-joint movements extensively, particularly the following lifts, which I term focus lifts:

Focus Lifts

1. Clean and Power Clean
2. Snatch and Power Snatch
3. Dead Lifts
4. Squats
5. Push Press and Push Jerk
6. Bench Press and
   Incline Press

These focus lifts are typically performed with traditional barbells or with the kettle bell variations and nonconforming objects, such as kegs and sandbags.

For ease of presentation, I use the following chart. It identifies the focus lifts along with hybrid and supplemental lifts and the different equipment/mediums that can be used. The focus lifts are then explained in the pages that follow. Additional supplemental lifts, such as general arm work, can also be added after having completed the regular program.

Chart of Lifting Movements

Focus Lifts	Equipment/ Mediums	Hybrid Lifts	Supplemental Lifts
Clean Power Clean	Kettlebells Barbells Kegs/Sandbags	Hang Clean Clean Pull Front Squat	Cuban Press Bent Rows Towel Chins
Snatch Power Snatch	Kettlebells Barbells Kegs/Sandbags	Hang Snatch Snatch Pull Overhead Squat Drop Snatch	
Dead lifts	Barbells Thick Bars	Turkish Get-Up	
Squats	Barbells	Lunges	Glute/Ham Raise Good Morning Reverse Hyper
Push Press Push Jerk	Kettlebells Barbells	Shoulder Press	Side Press
Bench press Incline press	Barbells Dumbbells		Rope Pulls Plate Raises Bradford Press

Renegade Training™
Copyright ©2002
John K. Davies
Dragon Door Publications, Inc.
1-800-899-5111
www.dragondoor.com

Kettlebell Lifts

Kettlebell work should be an instrumental portion of any lifting program and is a tremendously functional portion of the Renegade programs. Athletes who perform kettle bell lifts not only develop a superb understanding of muscular harmony and balance but also develop powerful tendons that are suitable for long-term strength work. Coaches find kettle bells an extraordinary medium, as it provides the perfect setting for training groups in an efficient manner. Kettlebell training is possibly one of the best mediums to vary strength training outside of use of barbells. Athletes are able to perform the motions of the Olympic lifts using the bell. Through the use of kettlebells the athletes can learn the proper hip thrust that will carry forward to not only other weight movements but sport specific functions on the field.

Olympic Lifts

The advantages of performing Olympic lifts are far reaching. In addition to serving as a tremendous method for improving power, doing Olympic lifts also improves balance and coordination and provides a useful ground-based activity.

For some unknown reason, performing Olympic lifts seems to have fallen out of favor among strength coaches. They are making a horrible mistake, as this is simply the finest approach available for developing the explosive power needed on the field of competition. Delving deeper into the program, you will notice that I also employ the full range of Olympic movements, which makes possible the tremendous compounding of exercises as well as the enhancing of neuromuscular traits.

1. Clean and Power Clean

To begin a clean lift, have the bar resting on the floor and your back in a neutral position (bent at 45 to 60 degrees). Grab the bar with your hands in an overhand grip, positioning them roughly shoulder width apart and the bar resting on the floor. The first pulling motion, which brings the bar to just above your knees, should be very controlled; keep your legs extended. The second pull should be initiated with your hips driving through and your knees rebending (known as the double-knee bend) as you move the bar up. Continue the thrust upward as your ankles, knees, and hips extend (known as triple extension). Catch the bar on the front of your shoulders by dropping under the bar, performing a full front squat, and rotating your elbows down and through the bar. The thrusting of hips up and through the bar completes the movement as the front squat is performed.

The Clean.

continued next page.

A power clean involves precisely the same motions, but instead of performing a full front squat, perform a dip under the bar.

The Power Clean.

continued next page.

The Kettlebell Power Clean.

2. Snatch and Power Snatch

Again, with the bar resting on the floor, grab the bar in an overhand grip. The width of the grip for the snatch can be easily determined: It's the distance from the outside of the elbow joint of the arm across the shoulders when your arms are held up to your sides. The first pulling motion to your knees should be very controlled. The second pulling motion is explosive, with the bar speeding to your hips with full extension. In another explosive movement, bring your outstretched arms overhead, supporting the weight while dropping into a full overhead squat.

If the lift is performed correctly, your outstretched body will appear somewhat like a bow, with your ankles in line with the back of your head. Fluidity of movement, not raw strength, is the key here. Even so, the lifter must be brutally strong in the legs and posterior chain. Pardon me for sounding so enthusiastic, but the snatch lift is a beautiful movement that exhibits a perfect balance of brutal power, speed, proprioception, and grace. It's a strength-training must for athletes!

The Snatch.

A power snatch is performed using the same motions, but instead of a full overhead squat, perform a dip under bar.

The Power Snatch.

3. Dead Lifts

The dead lift is possibly the most simple of all the focus lifts. To begin, align your feet flat beneath the bar and squat down to a neutral back position (i.e., 45 to 60 degrees), as in the clean lift. Grip the bar with your hands overlapping, one over and the other under. They should be shoulder width or slightly wider apart. Pull the bar up and over your head by fully extending your hips and knees. Throughout the lift, keep your hips low, your shoulders high, and your arms and back straight by pinching your rear delts back. Also keep the bar close to your body to improve mechanical leverage.

The Dead Lift.

4. Squats

Take the bar from the rack and, grasping it firmly, position it comfortably on the backs of your shoulders. Keep your head forward, your back straight, and your feet flat on the floor. With your feet in a wide stance (well outside shoulder width), begin the descent by pushing your buttocks backward. Continue to descend until your thighs are just past parallel to the floor. Once at this point, push upward by thrusting your hips forward and extending your body back to fully upright.

This method is often identified as the powerlifting squat or box squat. I use it because it concentrates on the power of the hips, glutes, and hamstrings. Bear in mind, however, that other squatting styles are used in Olympic lifts (see later in this chapter).

The Squat.

5. Push Press and Push Jerk

There are slight differences between the push press and push jerk, but both serve as the foundation of all overhead movements. Each starts with a slight dip that involves bending the knees, hips, and ankles somewhat. In the push jerk, lift the weight up in an explosive movement, extending your arms overhead while landing in a squat position, and then stand up. The push press begins with the same dip but with your legs straight. The other movements are the same as just described.

The Push Press.

With barbell supported in "rack" drop down to 1/4 squat position and begin exploding weight upwards.

Explode in a powerful jump upwards as feet leave ground.

Make powerful contact of feet to ground with legs straight and weight locked out above.

The Kettlebell Push Press.

The Push Jerk.

The Push Jerk can alternatively be performed with the movement intiated with bar on the shoulders as in a back squat..

Drop into 1/4 squat and explode the weight upwards.

As weight is exploding up, recoil back down to 1/4 squat position with arms locked-out above.

With kettlebell held firmly on "lat shelf", drop down to 1/4 squat position and begin exploding weight upwards.

Explode in a powerful jump upwards as feet leave ground.

The Kettlebell Push Jerk.

Make powerful contact of feet to ground with legs bent and weight locked out above.

Squat upwards with weight locked out.

6. Bench Press and Incline Press

These lifts are performed lying flat on your back on a weight bench, your feet flat on the floor. To begin, reach up and grasp the bar, keeping your rear delts pinched and your feet planted firmly on the floor. Your grip width should vary from shoulder width to one in which the elbow-to-wrist joint is 90 degrees to the bar at the bottom of the lift. Disengage the bar from the rack, and lower it to your chest at nipple level. Be sure to keep your elbows in tight, under control, and not bouncing. As the bar touches your chest, drive it upward in an explosive manner.

The Bench Press.

An interesting variation of the Bench by performing on a Swiss ball. Alternatively you can also perform with dumbbells on a Swiss ball. Pay particular caution with weight used because of the difficulty with stabilization.

When the incline press is performed with a barbell, a shoulder-width grip should be used to emulate hitting conditions on the field. The incline press can be performed on a dedicated or adjustable bench.

The Incline Bench Press.

An interesting variation of the Incline Bench by performing on a Swiss ball. Alternatively you can also perform with dumbbells on a Swiss ball. Pay particular caution with weight used because of the difficulty with stabilization.

Hybrid Lifts

1. Hang Clean
2. Clean Pull
3. Front Squat
4. Hang Snatch
5. Snatch Pull
6. Overhead Squat
7. Drop Snatch
8. Turkish Get-Up
9. Lunges
10. Shoulder Press

1. Hang Clean

This lift is performed using precisely the same motions as the clean lift, but its starts from a hang position at or below the knees. Start from a neutral position, with good back alignment, and use the standard overhead clean grip and stance. Lift the barbell upward in an explosive movement, extending your body. Keep the bar close to your body, shooting your elbows under the bar to catch it in the rack while simultaneously dropping underneath in a front squat position. When you turn your elbows underneath the bar and catch the weight, try to keep your elbows about parallel to the ground. The position of catching the bar is known as the rack. From this position, execute a front squat.

The Hang Clean.

2. Clean Pull

This is a simple clean lift but without the catch. Start with the bar on the floor, your back in good neutral position. Drive the weight off the ground, shrugging your shoulders to pull it upward.

The Clean Pull.

3. Front Squat

This is also a type of clean lift. Without making it seem too complex, a front squat is simply a barbell squat in which the weight is distributed on your chest. For the Olympic front squat, the bar is held with your hands in the rack. I mention the use of the hands because, as you may know, in Olympic lifting, the bar load is not necessarily on the wrists; the lifter often opens his or her hands to maintain position while the weight rests on his or her collarbone and shoulders. Because this position is naturally used in any clean-lifting motion, the lifter has the options of starting the movement from a squat rack or clean-lifting the weight up and then performing the front squat.

The Front Squat.

4. Hang Snatch

The hang snatch is precisely the same as the snatch, but it starts from a hang position at or below the knees.

The Hang Snatch.

5. Snatch Pull

This is a simple snatch but without the extension of the arms above the shoulders. Start with the bar on the floor, keeping your back in good neutral position. Drive the weight off the ground, shrugging your shoulders to pull the weight upward.

The Snatch Pull.

6. Overhead Squat

This lift, another type of snatch, is a tremendous movement for developing total body strength as well as balance and coordination. To begin, hold the bar above your head with a wide snatch grip, your feet hip-width apart. Lower the bar in a controlled fashion, and then raise it up again.

The Overhead Squat.

7. Drop Snatch

This is a superb lift that has definite benefits. Using a snatch grip, squat under the bar while it's still in the rack. Start the movement with a minor dip, and then lift the bar upward in an explosive movement. Drop into a full overhead squat as quickly as possible, your arms locked above your head, and then move up using the squat technique.

The Drop Snatch.

8. Turkish Get-Up

This is quite a simple lift that will thicken the torso. Lay on the floor, flat on your back. Holding a dumbbell in one hand, stretch that arm above your head with your elbow locked. Roll to one side and then stand up, still holding the dumbbell above your head. Once standing, reverse the movement.

The Turkish Get-Up.

Ensure control of body and that you maintain alignment throughout movement.

A powerful torso that becomes impenetrable!

9. Lunge

Begin in a standing position and with a barbell resting on your trapezius muscles behind your head. Step forward and down to the point that the knee of your rear leg gently makes contact with ground. Drive up to return to a standing position, and then repeat with the opposite leg.

The Lunge.

10. Shoulder Press

This lift is performed using a shoulder-width grip as you press the weight overhead with control. You can use a standing or seated position and lift barbells, dumbbells, kettle bells, or virtually any weighted objects.

The Shoulder Press.

Supplemental Lifts

1. Cuban Press
2. Bent Rows
3. Towel Chins
4. Glute/Ham Raise
5. Good Morning
6. Reverse Hyper
7. Side Press
8. Jump Shrugs
9. Plate Raises
10. Bradford Press

1. Cuban Press

This lift is best performed with dumbbells. Pinch your shoulders back and rotate your elbows up, keeping your shoulder to elbow joints parallel to the ground and your elbow to hand joints bent up at a 90-degree angle.

The Cuban Press.

2. Bent Rows

Begin from a bent-over position, using an overhand grip. Pull the bar to your chest, keeping your back straight.

The Bent Row.

3. Towel Chins

This simple chin lift is performed with a bar that has a towel draped over it.

The Towel Chin.

Toughen the grip up, throw a few towels over a bar and perform chin-ups!

4. Glute/Ham Raise

This lift can be performed either using a dedicated machine or on the floor using free weights. I recommend that you start training with a glute/ham machine, as this is a very difficult exercise. With your knees pressed against the pad, raise your body from the knee joints by driving up with your hamstrings and exerting pressure against the toe plate of the machine. To perform the lift on the floor, apply significant padding to the floor so your body is in biomechanic alignment similar to that of using the machine. Lower your body toward the floor, keeping your hips forward and your feet firmly planted. Then explode upward just before you touch the ground.

The Glute/Ham Raise.

The "natural" glute ham is by far the best manner to perform this movement – but it is the most challenging. With knees on a pad and heels held firmly down begin to lower torso the ground.

Ensure body is kept as straight as possible.

As hamstrings give out – allow body to come down to push out position and explode upward.

...but with only a slight amount of momentum until your hamstrings can pull yourself up.

5. Good Morning

The hamstrings, glutes, and spinal erectors get a great workout from this lift. It can be performed in a variety of ways, using a wide or narrow stance, a high or low bar, or even standing or seated. Squat under the bar, which is in a rack, and grab it using a firm grip. Keeping your back tight, initiate movement by pushing your buttocks backward and slightly bending your knees. Attain a neutral back position of 45 degrees, and raise up by pushing your hips forward.

The Good Morning.

6. Reverse Hyper

Do this lift using a dedicated machine or other apparatus, such as a pommel horse. With your upper torso resting parallel to ground and your legs straight down, bring your legs up to parallel position.

The Reverse Hyper.

Can also be performed using a Swiss ball. Many athletes tend to find this a more effective manner.

7. Side Press

Start with one hand holding a dumbbell or kettle bell at shoulder height and the other hand on your hip. Push the weight above your head as you straighten you arm and bend to the opposite side and then straighten up again.

The Side Press.

Now straight up by pushing hard with the obliques.

8. Jump Shrugs (Clean Grip and Snatch Grip)

The Jump Shrug (Clean Grip).

8. Jump Shrugs (Clean Grip and Snatch Grip)

The Jump Shrug (Snatch Grip).

The Kettlebell Jump Shrug.

9. Plate Raises

This lift can be performed either seated or standing. With the weight resting on your thighs (if standing) or your forearms against your inner thighs (if seated), grasp the plate at the 3 o'clock and 9 o'clock positions. Then lift the plate to eye level and back down again.

The Plate Raise.

10. Bradford Press

This is like the shoulder press, but you should only lift the weight to just above head level. From this position, rotate the bar until it touches front of your chest.

The Bradford Press.

Medicine Ball Lifts

Working with a medicine ball provides a simple training medium that both complements and extends other training areas: explosive training, core development, proprioreception, eye-hand coordination, and even sport-specific twisting actions, which are difficult to replicate using other methods. Even so, medicine ball training is another area that, for some reason, is often overlooked in many training programs. Again, this is a mistake. All training should involve movement of the neuromuscular system, and medicine ball work allows for superb range of movement. In addition, by varying the training load, medicine ball training can be used in a variety of ways: from enhancing recovery to improving maximal power output.

The Renegade programs use two basic circuits of medicine ball training. A ball weighing 3 to 5 kilograms maximum should be used. Many programs use a ball that is too heavy. The body is capable of maximum performance when it works in a harmonious balance. In completing the program, the athlete should move in a continuous fashion. Five throws should be done using each of 10 motions, for a total of 50 throws.

Medicine Ball Circuit A

1. Chest Pass
2. One-Hand Twisting Chest Pass (right forward)
3. One-Hand Twisting Chest Pass (left forward)
4. Step-In Chest Pass (right forward)
5. Step-In Chest Pass (left forward)
6. Overhead Pass
7. Walking Overhead Pass (right forward)
8. Walking Overhead Pass (left forward)
9. Scoop Forward
10. Scoop Backward

1. Chest Pass

With ball on chest, explode ball forward.

2. One-Hand Twisting Chest Pass (right forward)

With ball on shoulder of opposite hip and near hip facing target.

Explode ball forward exhibiting power from hip and torso movement.

3. One-Hand Twisting Chest Pass (left forward)

Repeat opposite side.

4. Step-In Chest Pass (right forward)

With ball on shoulder of opposite hip and near hip facing target.

Walk into pass with either leg (alternate)

5. Step-In Chest Pass (left forward)

Repeat opposite side.

6. Overhead Pass

Holding ball above head throw evenly distributed with both hands.

7. Walking Overhead Pass (right forward)

Walk into pass with either leg (alternate).

8. Walking Overhead Pass (left forward)

Repeat opposite side.

9. Scoop Forward

A simple yet great test of explosive strength. Hold ball at waist with legs spread.

Bend over and swing ball between legs.

Accelerate through throwing ball as powerfully as possible in front of you.

Momentum of throw should carry you forward into leap.

10. Scoop Backward

Essentially repeating the movements of Scoop Forward with a backward arch.

Bend over and swing ball between legs.

Accelerate through throwing ball as powerfully as possible directly behind you.

Medicine Ball Circuit B

1. Two-Hand Swing (R)
2. Two-Hand Swing (L)
3. One-Hand Swing (R)
4. One-Hand Swing (L)
5. Seated Throwing Twist (R)
6. Seated Throwing Twist (L)
7. Seated Twist (R)
8. Seated Twist (L)
9. Situp Pass
10. Torso Twist (count each touch to one side as 1 throw)

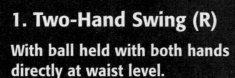

1. Two-Hand Swing (R)

With ball held with both hands directly at waist level.

Swing backwards, rotating body around.

Accelerate through, generating speed from hips.

2. Two-Hand Swing (L)

Repeat opposite side.

3. One-Hand Swing (R)

Holding ball in one hand swing back in discus like fashion

Generate speed and power from hips and torso as body rotates.

4. Two-Hand Swing (L)

Repeat opposite side.

5. Seated Throwing Twist (R)

Perform as in standing 2 handed swing.

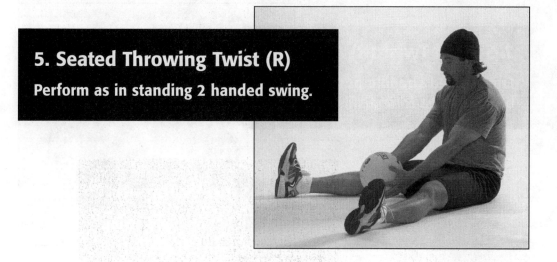

Rotate torso.

Swing through hard.

6. Seated Throwing Twist (L)

Repeat opposite side.

7. Seated Twist (R)

From seated straddle position, hold ball and twist to one side.

Place ball at back of hip.

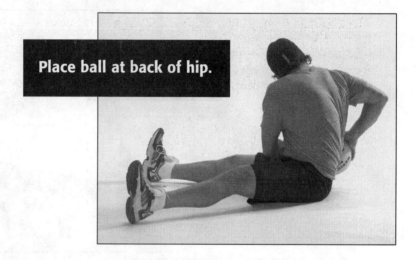

Twist back opposite way to retrieve ball.

8. Seated Twist (L)

Repeat opposite side.

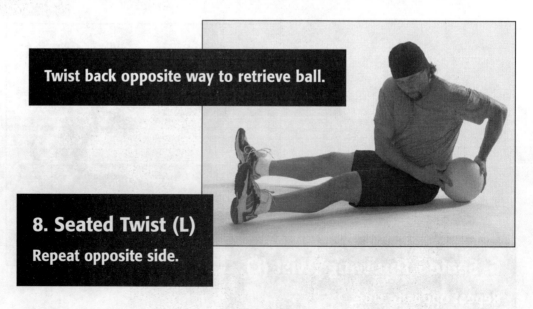

9. Situp Pass
Catch ball throw high.

with outstretched arms bring ball backwards.

touch ground and begin acceleration of throw forward.

Continue upwards with ball.

And throw.

10. Torso Twist (count each touch to one side as 1 throw)

Palms flat on ground, legs straight upright holding a ball.

Begin twisting to one side in controlled fashion.

slowly bring back to opposite side.

Abdominal Training

Rest assured, abdominal training is not an afterthought in the Renegade training plan, even though it appears here at the end of the chapter. In fact, the abs have been worked vigorously throughout the other training elements.

The abdominal carriage is involved in all aspects of football (and all other sports, for that matter). Movement on the field places tremendous pressure on this region; it's actually the center of all movement. For instance, speed is maximized with powerful arm drive that enhances swift and explosive leg action. A lack of abdominal strength will limit this ability tremendously. Having a weak abdominal core will cause poor technique and force production, as well.

Given the great demands made upon the trunk of the body, having a well-developed core is critical for athletic success. Maximum achievement on the field can only occur through development of the torso—namely, being able to maintain correct body position.

The carriage of the body should never be taken lightly in training. These exercises form the basis of Renegade abdominal training:

1. Leg Raises, Pike Position: Hanging from the high pullup bar, raise your straight legs upward to touch bar.
2. Leg Raises, Tuck Position: Hanging from the high pullup bar, raise your bent legs upward until your knees approach your chest area.
3. Reverse Crunches/Dragon Flags: Begin lying flat on a bench with your feet flat on the floor. Then curl your body upward until your knees are above eye level. Straighten your legs completely, and then slowly lower your body.
4. Chinees: Begin lying on the ground with your arms relaxed at your sides. Then move your legs in opposite movements. That is, while holding one leg flat on the ground, raise the opposite knee up to your torso and back down again. Repeat but alternate legs.
5. Pavelizer: maintain heel contact to ground, and squeezing glutes and hams tight. While slowly (i.e. 5 count) ascending squeeze abdominals tight and exert air from diaphram slowly. Finally at top expel all air and repeat going down.

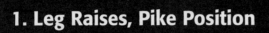

1. Leg Raises, Pike Position

Hanging from the high pullup bar, raise your straight legs upward to touch bar.

2. Leg Raises, Tuck Position

Tuck Position:
Hanging from the high pullup bar, raise your bent legs upward until your knees approach your chest area.

3. Reverse Crunches/Dragon Flags

Begin lying flat on a bench with your feet flat on the floor.

Then curl your body upward until your knees are above eye level.

Straighten your legs completely, and then slowly lower your body.

4. Chinees

Begin lying on the ground with your arms relaxed at your sides.

Then move your legs in opposite movements. That is, while holding one leg flat on the ground, raise the opposite knee up to your torso and back down again.

Repeat but alternate legs.

5. Pavelizer

The final element in Renegade abs training is the following abdominal circuit. Each of the 10 movements should be performed by touching the toes 10 times, for a total of 100 movements:

1. Legs Straight Up and Held Together
2. Legs Straight Up and Spread Apart
3. Legs Up in an "L" shape, bent at knees as if over a bench (touch 1 to 2 feet above the knees)
4. Standard Situp (touch 1 to 2 feet above the knees)
5. Side Sit (right side)
6. Side Sit (left side)
7. Standard Situp (touch 1 to 2 above the knees)
8. Legs Up in an "L" shape, bent at knees as if over a bench (touch 1 to 2 feet above the knees)
9. Legs Straight up and Spread Apart
10. Legs Straight Up and Held Together

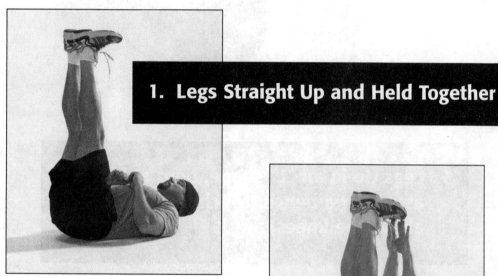

1. Legs Straight Up and Held Together

2. Legs Straight Up and Spread Apart

3. Legs Up in an "L" shape, bent at knees as if over a bench (touch 1 to 2 feet above the knees)

4. Standard Situp (touch 1 to 2 feet above the knees)

5. Side Sit (right side)

6. Side Sit (left side)

Chapter Five

Work Capacity Development

Throughout the previous chapters, I've laid out the basic tools needed to implement my Renegade blueprint for success. I contend that there is a pathway to greatness that, if followed, will lead an athlete toward his or her utmost potential. All to often, the failure of an athlete's development is simply the result of having a poor plan of attack—one that does not address the needs of the sport and the manner with which to achieve results. The result, ultimately, is the maddening "What if?" type of questioning of "what if" as well as unrealized or wasted potential. As I have noted on so many occasions, my greatest goal as a coach is to teach young athletes of seemingly common ability that they each possess an untapped source of physical talent.

I have placed work capacity development as the last topic in this book because I wanted first to impart to you those concepts needed at the start of training. To recap, those concepts are range of motion development, agility training, linear speed development, and strength development. Work capacity should be addressed later in your program, after you've laid a good foundation of these other skills.

In considering work capacity, you must first recognize the obvious: We are not all created equal in the physical sense. This is an absolute truth, regardless of what can be said about the nature of competition and personal drive. In fact, within organized sports, there is a so-called elite-level of athletes. A perfect example can be found in my own sport, football.

From high school, the best players advance to the collegiate level, mostly through the reward of an athletic scholarship. Throughout their collegiate experience, players refine and develop their technical skills while working diligently to improve their physical conditioning. A small percentage of these college-level players become standouts. And among this group of standouts, only some will have the opportunity to play at the professional level. The professional star is truly an exceptional athlete—an elite athlete, if you will.

In short, the "best of the best" advance, and all of the others are left behind. Yet interestingly enough, many of the top players at the collegiate level were not so highly regarded in high school. Evidence of this is easily found in the rosters of professional teams, which list many athletes from small schools and non–top 10 programs.

So, what does this say? Hard work is the real key to success. This notion has been the great motivating factor of my career. The challenge and focus of my work has not been to train the rare genetically gifted athlete but to develop the skills of the athletic with fewer innate gifts such that he or she can rise up and achieve above and beyond the loftiest of goals. Realizing that this is the mandate of Renegade Training, you may now have a better understanding of why the athlete's total physical and mental commitment is necessary for real success.

I began to formulate my personal theories of sport performance upon observing young athletes. Over the years, it has become readily apparent to me that American youth have suffered immeasurably due to the decline in active physical activities in both school and recreational programs. And when Americans' horrendous dietary habits are considered, as well—particularly the movement toward eating fast food—the situation is even worse. In fact, the epidemic of unhealthy young athletes has never been greater. This realization has led me to conclude that the central component of all training must be a remedy for this range of health problems. Thus, the theories I developed early on are still integral to my training programs.

General Physical Preparation (GPP)

Like a great building, athletic development must start with the construction of a solid foundation. While we can debate many complex issues of training, the need for a solid base cannot be disputed. All future development depends on it. At the base of my training is *General Physical Preparation*, or *GPP*. As the name implies, this is an element of training that balances the development of a variety of general physical skills, achieving the following results:

- Enhances motor skills
- Specifically trains for certain movement patterns that translate directly to sport-specific patterns
- Increases the work threshold, which in turn increases the level of fitness and sport preparation
- Promotes active physical recovery
- Promotes psychological regeneration for strenuous training
- Provides a conduit for the important transition to Specialized Physical Preparation, or SPP (which will be discussed further in the next section)

From another vantage, this aspect of training can have a positive influence on the athlete's psyche. As he or she is able to accomplish these tasks on a regular basis, an element of confidence will emerge along with the realization that taking a relentless "never say die" approach often reaps tremendous rewards. Within a team environment, this approach is arguably one of the best for building a unified, cohesive unit. Thus, it has been a staple of all military training, where team unity is a matter of utmost importance.

The specific activities performed in GPP are extremely diverse and virtually limitless, but to be effective, they must be completed in precise combinations. An assortment of weighted and nonweighted exercises are done on a daily basis for a period of time and according to a wave pattern of varying intensities—that is, short- and long-term periodization of varying workloads to gradually and scientifically build up work capacity.

Here is a sample pattern of nonweighted GPP exercises:

- Jumping Jacks
- Shuffle Splits
- Burpees
- Mountain Climbers

These simple movements should be completed with careful discipline. Each should be performed for at least 30 seconds in duration and with constant movement (i.e., no stopping).

Jumping Jacks

Perform with arms relatively straight and touch at top.

Ensure legs spread wide and come together – perform with discipline and show pride!

Shuffle Splits

Shuffle split back and forth with movement generated from hips.

Burpees

Jump up high with arms outstretched.

Down to your haunches.

Kick those legs back.

Bring feet back up with feet pointed straight ahead. Show power and speed! Now, do 15 per 30 seconds.

Mountain Climbers

From pushup type position, with one knee up near elbow and other outstretched.

Alternate "climbing" legs back & forth with speed. Ensure feet and knees always point straight ahead.

Weighted GPP exercises include a wide assortment of drills, such as those in this sample:

- Wheelbarrow Drags
- Farmer's Walk
- Pulling Sled/Tire Walk
- Pulling Sled/Tire Straight Leg Drag
- Pulling Sled/Tire Walk with Arms Outstretched

As with nonweighted GPP, weighted training is done with a time factor (i.e., at least 30 seconds of constant movement per exercise) and follows a wave pattern of varying intensities. The intensity should follow a pattern in which ballistic and semiballistic types of exercise (e.g., squat thrusts and burpees) alternate with active types (e.g., jumping jacks and shuffle splits). As the athlete's level of fitness improves, he or she should work on the ability to perform while recovering from exercise. In short, weighted GPP offers the athlete a unique training opportunity.

Combative Work

One area that is paramount to the successful performance of athletes is combative training, or the use of contact and hand strikes, which can be classified as a type of SPP. For players at all positions of the game (excluding quarterback), hand strikes and the speed at which they're delivered often result in making tackles made and thus decide the flow of the game. Most training programs fail to recognize this, however. In fact, combative training is possibly the most overlooked facet of specialized physical preparation in football. As a result, most players stay clear of these drills from the end of the season until the start of training camp. For the football player to ignore this component of training is tantamount to a boxer not practicing punches or not hitting a bag for two-thirds of the year.

Renegade Training uses some basic punch patterns to reinforce the speed and explosiveness as well as to improve technical proficiency. The repetition involved in punch work will make athletes comfortable in their game functions and allow them to operate in reflex mode.

The punch pattern can easily be performed by striking a bag or pad. Strikes should be performed from a positional stance against a padded wall surface or using a stable dummy on weight-training days with pushing motions. Using the ladder approach outlined below—in which each set adds 5 punches per pattern, or 50 punches total—is a great way to increase the total strike count. Pay careful attention to the athlete's stance; he or she should strike in a quick action and then recoil, moving his or her hands back into position as quickly as possible to prepare for the next strike. In advanced stages, athletes should also perform the routine blindfolded to enhance their sensory patterns.

Punch Pattern	5-punch ladder	10-punch ladder	15-punch ladder	20-punch ladder
Right jab	5	10	15	20
Left jab	5	10	15	20
Double-punch	10	20	30	40
Combo: Right, right, left	15	30	45	60
Combo: Left, left, right	15	30	45	60
Total strikes per set	50	100	150	200

Renegade Training™
Copyright ©2002
John K. Davies
Dragon Door Publications, Inc.
1-800-899-5111
www.dragondoor.com

Chapter Six

Spiritual Development

The athlete who is intent on being successful follows the proverbial "road less traveled." The pathway to greatness exists, but only those who have conviction in their goals will complete the journey. While a handful of athletes are blessed with rare genetic gifts that elicit the perception that they are special, I prefer to think of those individuals who dedicate themselves to preparation and attack their loftiest of goals as the special ones. The athletes who continue to push themselves when others slack off or drop out—they are truly the gifted ones.

Throughout this book, I have laid a blueprint for how to fulfill an athlete's physical potential in training for the football field. Yet in this final chapter, I must turn to the athlete's spiritual potential, for his or her degree of commitment will go a long way in determining success. In fact, it may be the first step along the pathway to greatness.

What is the source of that commitment? What determines an athlete's resolve or motivation? An attempt to answer these questions would likely stir up the age-old debate of nature versus nurture. A selected few athletes seem born to play their sport and come equipped with the physical skills and psychological determination to make it happen. Others are raised with a strong work ethic, but that is becoming more and more rare, unfortunately. Thus, training needs to take on the additional purpose of developing the "never say die" attitude that is required to excel. Regardless of talent, the greatest gift any athlete can possess is that of want and desire.

In my coaching experience, I've proven that this relentless attitude can be fostered among athletes, but first, the will and desire must be there. The athletes I've trained are so accustomed to being challenged that overcoming adversity in performance is significantly easier for them. To be successful on the field, athletes must have intimate knowledge of how to deal with chaotic environments and how to react instinctively. This is basically a military theory that I adapted for my training programs a long time ago, and the success of my programs has proven its validity.

Will and desire set the foundation of all training, for without the proper psychological development, all physical development will be fruitless. In addition, the following personal attributes are needed to achieve greatness. They are all intertwined and thus mutually dependent and reinforcing. These attributes are genderless, ageless, and without racial or economic barriers:

Integrity:
Strict adherence to a code of ethics or a standard of behavior

This is the moral fabric of the athlete and thus impacts his or her drive, commitment, and discipline. Qualities such as passion, restraint, and interpersonal skills help form the cornerstone of the spirit of an athlete. These qualities will pay rich dividends during those tough training periods in which the athlete must respond to a challenge.

Drive:
The insatiable and relentless thirst to succeed

This is perhaps the most important quality an athlete can have. The successful athlete makes progress most efficiently by focusing on and working toward well-thought-out goals. True drive is unyielding, even in the face of real adversity. One cannot quit until the mission has been accomplished. There is no task that cannot be completed.

Commitment:
A pledge to fulfill a particular purpose of course of action.

Renegade Training takes athletes through a comprehensive and brutal workout, in which they are challenged at every turn. And in the event they do not have the resolve to finish, I will drag their carcasses up to complete the session! My point in doing so is to teach them that an athlete—a great athlete—can never be vanquished. I realize that exercise physiologists will criticize this approach as unsound. And they may be right, except for one thing: My athletes learn to defy the challenges set before them, and that learning starts right here! Some might consider this approach as punishment, but that's not my intent. My goal is to make every athlete better, stronger, and tougher mentally as well as physically. Pain not only will be denied, but it will become an ally. Losing cannot be considered an option.

Discipline:
Strict adherence to a system of rules that govern conduct or activity.

The disciplined athlete is so committed to achieving his or her goals that he or she considers even those elements beyond training, such as diet and rest. In sum, training must extend to all aspects of one's life that will improve performance. The comprehensive element of discipline is something many athletes do not understand when they commit themselves to training.

Conviction: A strongly held belief or attitude. Conviction may also be called faith, but not as it's used in the religious sense. Rather, the appropriate meaning of faith for this context is that from the motto of the U.S. Marine Corps, "Semper fidelis," which is Latin for "always faithful." The athlete who possesses real conviction will have the courage and perseverance to press on during the most difficult times because he or she will know that this it the right course of action.

Making your way along the pathway to greatness is unquestionably a daunting task. But every journey must begin by taking that first step. For the athlete, that first step is to develop his or mindset—namely, the will and desire to achieve. With that as the foundation for the development of the requisite physical skills, an athlete is surely destined for success.

So, in the very simplest of terms, take control of your destiny. Seize and crush every limitation you see before you.

About the Author

Coach Davies develops comprehensive training packages for all facets and levels of football, from high school to college to the NFL. Internationally, Coach Davies has been acclaimed for his work with European and South America soccer teams.

His Renegade Training philosophy is controversial but has proved highly successful in application. According to Coach Davies:

"The sheer brutality of my work is probably the reason why my work is so controversial. My approach to work thresholds is unquestionably the crux of arguments against my training philosophy. My athletes are constantly reminded of the relentless, violent nature of their sport and our training reflects that.

Football in its purest form can be simply explained as a sport played by enormous men, of tremendous strength at an alarmingly fast pace. You must prepare your body and mind for the battle ahead. Preparation quickly decides who are the victors and the vanquished. I do not merely ask a lot of my athletes, I ask more than they ever imagined."

Coach Davies instills a "warrior mindset" in his athletes. The result: a stand-out toughness capable of excelling in the controlled chaos and extreme stress of modern football. Physically, his athletes have consistently broken through past performance barriers to dramatically enhance their speed, strength and power.

To contact the author directly email Coach Davies at:

coachdavies@renegadetraining.com

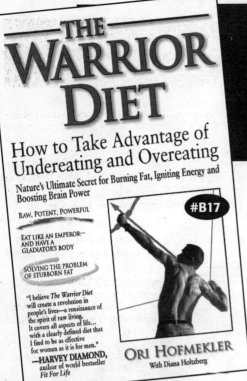

The Warrior Diet
How to Take Advantage of Undereating and Overeating

Nature's Ultimate Secret for Burning Fat, Igniting Energy and Boosting Brain Power
By Ori Hofmekler
With Diana Holtzberg

Hardcover 5 3/8" x 8 3/8", 420 pages,
Over 150 photographs and illustrations
Item #B17   **$26.95**

Eat like an emperor–and have a gladiator's body

Are you still confused about what, how and when to eat? Despite the diet books you have read and the programs you have tried, do you still find yourself lacking in energy, carrying excess body fat, and feeling physically run-down? Sexually, do you feel a shadow of your former self?

The problem, according to **Ori Hofmekler,** is that we have lost touch with the natural wisdom of our instinctual drives. We have become the slaves of our own creature comforts— scavenger/victims rather than predator/victors. When to comes to informed-choice, we lack any real sense of personal freedom. The result: ill-advised eating and lifestyle habits that leave us vulnerable to all manner of disease—not to mention obesity and sub-par performance.

The Warrior Diet presents a brilliant and far-reaching solution to our nutritional woes, based on a return to the primal power of our natural instincts.

The first step is to break the chains of our current eating habits. Drawing on a combination of ancient history and modern science, *The Warrior Diet* proves that humans are at their energetic, physical, mental and passionate best when they "undereat" during the day and "overeat" at night. Once you master this essential eating cycle, a new life of explosive vigor and vitality will be yours for the taking.

Unlike so many dietary gurus, Ori Hofmekler has personally followed his diet for over twenty-five years and is a perfect model of *the Warrior Diet's* success— the man is a human dynamo.

Not just a diet, but a whole way of life, *the Warrior Diet* encourages us to seize back the pleasures of being alive—from the most refined to the wild and raw. *The Warrior Diet* is practical, tested, and based in commonsense. Expect results!

The Warrior Diet covers all the bases. As an added bonus, discover delicious Warrior Recipes, a special Warrior Workout, and a line of Warrior Supplements—designed to give you every advantage in the transformation of your life from average to exceptional.

About Ori Hofmekler

Ori Hofmekler is a modern Renaissance man whose life has been driven by two passions: art and sports. Hofmekler's formative experience as a young man with the Israeli Special Forces, prompted a lifetime's interest in diets and fitness regimes that would optimize his physical and mental performance.

After the army, Ori attended the Bezalel Academy of Art and the Hebrew University, where he studied art and philosophy and received a degree in Human Sciences.

A world-renowned painter, best known for his controversial political satire, Ori's work has been featured in magazines worldwide, including *Time, Newsweek, Rolling Stone, People, The New Republic* as well as *Penthouse* where he was a monthly columnist for 17 years and Health Editor from 1998–2000. Ori has published two books of political art, *Hofmekler's People,* and *Hofmekler's Gallery.*

As founder, Editor-In-Chief, and Publisher of *Mind & Muscle Power,* a national men's health and fitness magazine, Ori introduced his Warrior Diet to the public in a monthly column—to immediate acclaim from readers and professionals in the health industry alike.

NUTRITION AND FITNESS EXPERTS IN STAMPEDE TO ENDORSE BENEFITS OF THE WARRIOR DIET

"In my quest for a lean, muscular body, I have seen practically every diet and suffered through most of them. It is also my business to help others with their fat loss programs. I am supremely skeptical of any eating plan or "diet" book that can't tell me how and why it works in simple language. Ori Hofmekler's *The Warrior Diet* does just this, with a logical, readable approach that provides grounding for his claims and never asks the reader to take a leap of faith. *The Warrior Diet* can be a very valuable weapon in the personal arsenal of any woman."

—DC Maxwell, 2-time Women's Brazilian Jiu-Jitsu World Champion, Co-Owner, Maxercise Sports/Fitness Training Center and Relson Gracie Jiu-Jitsu Academy East

"The credo that has served me well in my life and that which I tell my patients is that I only take advice from those who practice what they preach. To me, there is nothing more pathetic and laughable than to see the terrible physical condition of many of the self-proclaimed diet and fitness experts of today. Those hypocrites who do not live by their own words are not worth your time, or mine.

At the other extreme, Ori Hofmekler is the living, breathing example of a warrior. There is real strength in the sinews of his muscle. There is wisdom and power in his words. His passion for living honestly is intense and reflective of the toil of a tough army life. Yet in a fascinating and true Spartan way, his physical nature is tempered by an equal reveling in the love of art, knowledge of the classic poets, and in the drinking of fine wine with good conversation.

Welcome *The Warrior Diet* into your life and you usher in the honest and real values of a man who has truly walked the walk. He has treaded the dirt of the path that lay before you, and is thus a formidable guide to a new beginning. He is your shepherd of integrity that will lead you out of the bondage of misinformation. His approach is what I call "revolutionarily de-evolutionary". In other words, your freedom from excess body fat, flat energy levels, and poor physical performance begins with unlearning the modern ways, which have failed you, and forging a new understanding steeped in the secret traditions of the ancient Roman warrior."

—Carlon M. Colker, M.D., F.A.C.N., author of *The Greenwich Diet*, CEO and Medical Director, Peak Wellness, Inc.

"*The Warrior Diet* certainly defies so-called modern nutritional and training dogmas. Having met Ori on several occasions, I can certainly attest that he is the living proof that his system works. He maintains a ripped muscular body year round despite juggling extreme workloads and family life. His take on supplementation is refreshing as he promotes an integrated and timed approach. *The Warrior Diet* is a must read for the nutrition and training enthusiast who wishes to expand his horizons."

—Charles Poliquin, author of *The Poliquin Principles* and *Modern Trends in Strength Training*, Three-Time Olympic Strength Coach

"Despite its name, *The Warrior Diet* isn't about leading a Spartan lifestyle, although it is about improving quality of life. With a uniquely compelling approach, the book guides you towards the body you want by re-awakening primal instinct and biofeedback—the things that have allowed us to evolve this far.

Ironically, in a comfortable world of overindulgence, your survival may still be determined by natural selection. If this is the case, *The Warrior Diet* will be the only tool you'll need."

—Brian Batcheldor, Science writer/researcher, National Coach, British Powerlifting Team

"In a era of decadence, where wants and desires are virtually limitless, Ori's vision recalls an age of warriors, where success meant survival and survival was the only option. A diet of the utmost challenge from which users will reap tremendous benefits."

—John Davies, Olympic and professional sports strength/speed coach

"Ori Hofmekler has his finger on a deep, ancient and very visceral pulse—one that too many of us have all but forgotten. Part warrior-athlete, part philosopher-romantic, Ori not only reminds us what this innate, instinctive rhythm is all about, he also shows us how to detect and rekindle it in our own bodies. His program challenges and guides each of us to fully reclaim for ourselves the strength, sinew, energy and spirit that humans have always been meant to possess."

—Pilar Gerasimo, Editor in Chief, *Experience Life Magazine*

"Ori and I became friends and colleagues in 1997 when he so graciously took me under his wing as a writer for *Penthouse* Magazine and *Mind and Muscle Power*.

When I received *The Warrior Diet* in the mail I nearly burst with pride. Not only because my dear friend had finally reached his particular goal of helping others be the best they can be physically, but because I had a small role in the creation of the book. Ori enlisted my help in researching topics such as the benefits of fasting, the perfect protein, and glycogen loading. I believe in Ori's concepts because I trust him wholeheartedly and because I helped uncover the scientific data that proves them. I also live by *The Warrior Diet*, although not to the extreme that Ori does. My body continues to get tighter and more toned in all of the right places...and people marvel at my eating practices.

Read *The Warrior Diet* with an open mind. Digest the information at your own pace. Assimilate the knowledge to make it fit into your current lifestyle. You will be amazed at how much more productive and energetic you will be. Be a warrior in your own right. Your body will thank you for it."

—Laura Moore, Science writer, *Penthouse* Magazine, *IronMan* Magazine, Body of the Month for IronMan, Sept 2001, Radio Talk Show Host *The Health Nuts*, author of *Sex Heals*

1•800•899•5111
24 HOURS A DAY
FAX: (970) 872-3862

POWER TO THE PEOPLE!

RUSSIAN STRENGTH TRAINING SECRETS FOR EVERY AMERICAN

By Pavel Tsatsouline

8½" x 11" 124 pages, over 100 photographs and illustrations—$34.95 #B10

How would you like to own a world class body—<u>whatever your present condition</u>— by doing only two exercises, for twenty minutes a day?" A body so lean, ripped and powerful looking, you won't believe your own reflection when you catch yourself in the mirror.

And what if you could do it without a single supplement, without having to waste your time at a gym and with only a 150 bucks of simple equipment?

And how about not only being stronger than you've ever been in your life, but having higher energy and better performance in whatever you do?

How would you like to have an instant download of the world's <u>absolutely most effective strength secrets?</u> To possess exactly the same knowledge that created world-champion athletes—and the strongest bodies of their generation?"

Pavel Tsatsouline's *Power to the People!— Russian Strength Training Secrets for Every American* delivers all of this and more.

As **Senior Science Editor for Joe Weider's *Flex* magazine, Jim Wright** is recognized as one of the world's premier authorities on strength training. Here's more of what he had to say:

Here's just some of what you'll discover, when you possess your own copy of Pavel Tsatsouline's *Power to the People!*:

- How to get super strong without training to muscle failure or exhaustion
- How to hack into your 'muscle software' and magnify your power and muscle definition
- How to get super strong <u>without putting on an ounce of weight</u>
- Or how to build massive muscles with a classified Soviet Special Forces workout
- Why high rep training to the 'burn' is like a form of rigor mortis— and what it really takes to develop spectacular muscle tone
- How to mold your whole body into an off-planet rock with only two exercises
- How to increase your bench press by ten pounds overnight
- How to get a tremendous workout on the road without any equipment
- How to design a world class body in your basement—with $150 worth of basic weights and in twenty minutes a day
- How futuristic techniques can squeeze more horsepower out of your body-engine
- How to maximize muscular tension for traffic-stopping muscular definition
- How to minimize fatigue and get the most out of your strength training
- How to ensure high energy after your workout
- How to get stronger and harder without getting bigger
- Why it's safer to use free weights than machines
- How to achieve massive muscles <u>and </u>awesome strength—if that's what you want
- What, how and when to eat for maximum gains
- How to master the magic of effective exercise variation
- The ultimate formula for strength
- How to gain beyond your wildest dreams—with less chance of injury
- A high intensity, immediate gratification technique for massive strength gains
- The eight most effective breathing habits for lifting weights
- The secret that separates elite athletes from 'also-rans'
- How to become super strong and live to tell about it

> *"You are not training if you are not training with Pavel!"*
>
> —Dr. Fred Clary, National Powerlifting Champion and World Record Holder.

Russians have always made do with simple solutions without compromising the results. NASA aerospace types say that while America sends men to the moon in a Cadillac, Russia manages to launch them into space in a tin can. Enter the tin can approach to designing a world class body—in your basement with $150 worth of equipment. After all, US gyms are stuffed with hi-tech gear, yet it is the Russians with their metal junkyard training facilities who have dominated the Olympics for decades.

POWER TO THE PEOPLE!

Russian Strength Training Secrets For Every American

With Pavel Tsatsouline

#V102

POWER TO THE PEOPLE

By Pavel Tsatsouline
Video, Running time: 47 min
$29.95   #V102

Praise for Pavel's Power to the People!

POWER TO THE PEOPLE!

By Pavel Tsatsouline

Russian Strength Training Secrets For Every American

#B10

"In **Power to the People!** Pavel Tsatsouline reveals an authen tically Russian approach to physical fitness. He shows how anyone, by learning how to contract their muscles harder, can build up to incredible levels of strength without gaining an ounce of weight. He shows how to exercise with a super-strict form and lift more weight than can be accomplished by swing or cheat. Now it's possible to train the human body to world-class fitness standards at home, working out for twenty minutes a day, and with only $150.00 worth of basic weights. **Power to the People!** is a highly recommended addition to any personal or professional physical fitness reference bookshelf."—**Midwest Book Review, Oregon, WI**

Brash and insightful, Power to the People is a valuable compilation of how-to strength training information. Pavel Tsatsouline offers a fresh and provocative perspective on resistance training, and charts a path to self-improvement that is both practical and elegantly simple. If building strength is your top priority, then *Power to the People* belongs at the top of your reading list. —**Rob Faigin, author of Natural Hormonal Enhancement**

"I learned a lot from Pavel's books and plan to use many of his ideas in my own workouts. *Power to the People!* is an eye-opener. It will give you new—and valuable—perspectives on strength training. You will find plenty of ideas here to make your training more productive."—**Clarence Bass, author of Ripped 1, 2 &3.**

"A good book for the athlete looking for a routine that will increase strength without building muscle mass. Good source of variation for anyone who's tired of doing standard exercises."—**Jonathan Lawson, IronMan Magazine**

"I have been a training athlete for over 30 years. I played NCAA basketball in college, kick boxed as a pro for two years, made it to the NFL as a free agent in 1982, powerlifted through my 20's and do Olympic lifting now at 42. I have also coached swimming and strength athletes for over 20 years.I have never read a book more useful than **Power to the People!** I have seen my strength explode like I was in my 20's again—and my joints are no longer hurting."—**Carter Stamm, New Orleans, LA**

"I have been following a regimen I got from *Power to the People!* for about seven weeks now. I have lost about 17lbs and have lost three inches in my waist. My deadlift has gone from a meager 180lbs to 255 lbs in that short time as well."—**Lawrence J. Kochert**

"Like *Beyond Stretching* and *Beyond Crunches*, his other books, this is great. I think that it is the best book on effective strength training that I have ever read. This is not a book just about theory and principles. But Tsatsouline provides a detailed and complete outline of an exact program to do and how to customize it for yourself. It is very different from anything you have probably every read about strength training. The things he teaches in the book though won't just get you strong, if you want more than that, but can make you look really good—lean, ripped, and/or real big muscled if you want it. It's a very good book; the best available English-language print matter on the topic of strength training."—**Dan Paltzik**

"The great thing about the book *"Power to the People!"* is that it tells the readers what not to do when training for strength and why not. As you read the book, you will keep saying to yourself: "so that's why I'm not getting stronger!" Pavel points out all the things that are wrong with conventional weight training (and there is lots of it) and shows the readers what they need to do to get stronger, but not necessarily bigger."— **Sang Kim, Rome, GA**

"Using Pavel Tsatsouline's weight training methods from his book *Power to the People* gives you the feeling that you can take on the world after only a 20-30 minute workout! Tsatsouline's book is written with such cleverness, clarity, and detail that I couldn't put it down. I am thoroughly enthusiastic about weight training where my past indoor training consisted only of Yoga postures. I would recommend this book to anyone interested in enhancing their performance on the job, in weight training, and in other athletic pursuits.

Pavel's genius is that he can take a complex subject like weight training and design a program that is enjoyable, efficient and gets fast results. He has done the same thing for abdominal development and stretching."—**Cliff D.V., Honolulu, Hawaii**

"I have experienced Pavel Tsatsouline's methods up close and in person, and his scientific approach lays waste to the muscleheaded garbage that we've been conditioned to follow. Pavel will show you how to achieve a full-body workout with just two core exercises and $150 worth of barbell equipment. You won't get injured and you won't get stiff. You'll just get what you were looking for in the first place - a program that works and one that you'll stick with." — **David M Gaynes, Bellevue, WA**

"It isn't growth hormone... it's Pavel! This is THE definitive text on the art and science of strength training... and that's what it's all about, power! Page after page of the world's most useful and productive strength-training practices are explained in this book. A lot of experienced lifters, who think that they know how to train, will be humbled when they find out how much better Pavel's system is than anything the western iron-game community has ever done. I have surpassed all my previous bests...and I no longer need or use lifting belts. I learned how to up-regulate tension through his "feed-forward" technique, how to i mmediately add AT LEAST ten pounds to every lift via "hyperirradiation", and to do it in my best form ever, and how to gain on every lift WEEKLY through the Russian system of periodization without any plateaus! Seriously, I gain every week! You only need TWO exercises! Pavel explains which ones, how to do them and how often. Also, you'll learn how to train to SUCCESS, not to "failure", how to immediately turn any lift into a "hyper lift", teach your nervous system how not to ever "miss" a lift, and simultaneously make your body far less injury-prone! Pavel illustrates the two types of muscle growth and which one you REALLY need, and the all-important power breathing. Pavel's training is the most valuable resource made available for strength athletes since the barbell. The breathing techniques alone are worth the asking price. This book is my personal favorite out of all his works, and in my opinion, they should be owned as a set. This book is superior to all the muscle mags and books that dwell on a content of unessential details of today's "fitness culture" and yet never fully explain the context of training for strength. Pavel cuts right to the heart of the "muscle mystery", by explaining the all-important context of the Russian system: quick, efficient, permanent strength gains, without spending a small fortune on "me-too" bodybuilding supplements and without unnecessary, time consuming overtraining. Now I only hope he writes a book on full-contact training..."—**Sean Williams, Long Beach, NY**

"This is a real source of no-b.s. information on how to build strength without adding bulk. I learned some new things which one can't find in books like *'Beyond Brawn'* or *'Dinosaur Training'*. Perhaps an advanced powerlifter, who reads Milo, already knows all that stuff, but I would definitely recommend this book to everyone from beginners to intermediates who are interested in increasing their strength." —**Nikolai Pastouchenko, Tallahassee, Florid**

"Forget all of the fancy rhetoric. If you are serious about improving your strength and your health buy this book and pay attention to what's provided. I started in January 2000 doing deadlifts with 200 lbs. Three months later I was at 365 lbs. Pavel knows what he is talking about and knows how to explain it simply. That's it."—**Alan, Indiana**

The Russian Kettlebell Challenge
Xtreme Fitness for Hard Living Comrades

with Pavel Tsatsouline, Master of Sports

The Russian Kettlebell Challenge

Xtreme Fitness for Hard Living Comrades

with Pavel Tsatsouline, Master of Sports

Item # V103 $39.95

Video Running Time: 32 minutes

An ancient Russian exercise device, the kettlebell has long been a favorite in that country for those seeking a special edge in strength and endurance.

It was the key in forging the mighty power of dinosaurs like Ivan "the Champion of Champions", Poddubny. Poddubny, one of the strongest men of his time, trained with kettlebells in preparation for his undefeated wrestling career and six world champion belts.

Many famous Soviet weightlifters, such as Vorobyev, Vlasov, Alexeyev, and Stogov, started their Olympic careers with old-fashioned kettlebells.

Kettlebells come in "poods". A pood is an old Russian measure of weight, which equals 16kg, or 36 pounds. There are one, one and a half, and two pood K-bells, 16, 24, and 32kg respectively.

To earn his national ranking, Pavel Tsatsouline had to power snatch a 32kg kettlebell forty times with one arm, and forty with the other back to back and power clean and jerk two such bells forty-five times.

Soviet science discovered that repetition kettlebell lifting is one of the best tools for all around physical development. (Voropayev, 1983) observed two groups of college students over a period of a few years. A standard battery of the armed forces PT tests was used: pullups, a standing broad jump, a 100m sprint, and a 1k run. The control groupfollowed the typical university physical training program which was military oriented and emphasized the above exercises. The experimental group just lifted kettlebells. In spite of the lack of practice on the tested drills, the KB group showed better scores in every one of them.

The Red Army, too pragmatic to waste their troopers, time on pushups and situps, quickly caught on. Every Russian military unit's gym was equipped with K-bells. Spetznaz, Soviet Special Operations, personnel owe much of their wiry strength, explosive agility, and never quitting stamina to kettlebells. High rep C&Js and snatches with K-bells kick the fighting man,s system into warp drive.

In addition to their many mentioned benefits, the official kettlebell lifts also develop the ability to absorb ballistic shocks. If you want to develop your ability to take impact try the
official K-bell lifts. The repetitive ballistic shock builds extremely strong tendons and ligaments.

The ballistic blasts of kettlebell lifting become an excellent conditioning tool for athletes from rough sports like kick boxing, wrestling, and football. And the extreme metabolic cost of high rep KB workouts will put your unwanted fat on a

If you are looking for a supreme edge in your chosen sport—seek no more!

Both the Soviet Special Forces and numerous world-champion Soviet Olympic athletes used the ancient Russian Kettlebell as their secret weapon for xtreme fitness. Thanks to the kettlebells's astonishing ability to turbocharge physical performance, these Soviet supermen creamed their opponents time-and-time-again, with inhuman displays of raw power and explosive strength.

Now, former Spetznaz trainer, international fitness author and nationally ranked kettlebell lifter, Pavel Tsatsouline, delivers this secret Soviet weapon into your own hands.

You NEVER have to be second best again! Here is the first-ever complete kettlebell training program—for Western shock-attack athletes who refuse to be denied—and who'd rather be dead than number two.

- **Get really, really nasty—with a commando's wiry strength, the explosive agility of a tiger and the stamina of a world-class ironman.**

- **Own the single best conditioning tool for killer sports like kickboxing, wrestling, and football.**

- **Watch in amazement as high-rep kettlebells let you hack the fat off your meat—without the dishonor of aerobics and dieting**

- **Kick your fighting system into warp speed—with high-rep snatches and clean-and-jerks**

- **Develop steel tendons and ligaments—and a whiplash power to match**

- **Effortlessly absorb ballistic shocks—and laugh as you shrug off the hardest hits your opponent can muster**

- **Go ape on your enemies—with gorilla shoulders and tree-swinging traps**

Announcing: "The World's *Single Most Effective Tool* for Massive Gains in Strength, Speed and Athletic Endurance"

Discover why **Russian Kettlebells** are storming into "favored status" with US military, SWAT, NFL, MLB, powerlifters, weightlifters, martial artists—and <u>elite athletes everywhere.</u>

"Kettlebells are unsurpassed as a medium for increasing strength and explosive power. Thanks to Pavel Tsatsouline, I have now rewritten my training program to include kettlebell training, for athletes of all disciplines from Professional Football to Olympic sprinters."
—*Coach John Davies*

Each authentic Russian Kettlebell is manufactured exclusively by Dragon Door Publications in traditional weight sizes. The kettlebells are made out of solid cast iron and are coated in the highest quality scratch and rust resistant cathodic epoxy gloss. These kettlebells are designed to last a lifetime—and beyond.

Special warning: the *Russian Kettlebell* is an *Xtreme Edge Fitness* Tool for serious workout fiends. It is not a Barbie toy! Treat your kettlebell lifting with the utmost care, precision and respect. Watch Pavel's kettlebell video many, many times for perfect form and correct execution. If possible, sign up for one of Pavel's upcoming Kettlebell Training Bootcamp/ Certification programs. Lift at your own discretion! We are not responsible for you boinking yourself on the head, dropping it on your feet or any other politically-incorrect action. Stick to the Party line, Comrade!

- Get thick, cable-like, hellaciously hard muscle
- Get frightening, whip-like speed
- Get stallion-like staying-power in any sport
- Get a, well, <u>god-like</u> physique
- Get the most brutal workout of your life, without having to leave your own living room
- Get a jack-rabbit's jumping power—and a jack-hammer's strength
- Get it all—and then more, with Russian KB's
- Get way more energy in way less time

NEW 40kg/88lb Kettlebell

MANUFACTURED IN AMERICA

88 lb.   70 lb.   53 lb.   35 lb.

#P10A	Russian Kettlebell—16kg (approx. 35lb)	$89.95
#P10B	Russian Kettlebell—24kg (approx. 53lb)	$109.95
#P10C	Russian Kettlebell—32kg (approx. 70lb)	$139.95
#P10F	Russian Kettlebell—40kg (approx. 88lb)	$179.95
#SP10	Russian Kettlebell—Set, one of A, B & C 16, 24 & 32kg. (Save $17.00)	$322.85

Shipping Charges

#P10A	Russian Kettlebell—16kg	SH: $24.00
#P10B	Russian Kettlebell—24kg	SH: $32.00
#P10C	Russian Kettlebell—32kg	SH: $39.00
#P10F	Russian Kettlebell—40kg	SH: $52.00
#SP10	Russian Kettlebell Set of A, B & C	SH: $95.00

The Russian Kettlebells are only available to customers resident in the U.S. mainland. Normal shipping charges do not apply. No rush orders on kettlebells. See chart above for shipping charges.

Here's what you'll discover, when you possess your own copy of Pavel Tsatsouline's The Russian *Kettlebell Challenge—Xtreme Fitness for Hard Living Comrades*

The Russian Kettlebell Challenge— Xtreme Fitness for Hard Living Comrades

By Pavel Tsatsouline   **#B15**

Paperback   170 pages   **$34.95**

Section One
The History of the Russian Kettlebell—How and Why a Low-Tech Ball of Iron Became the National Choice for Super-Tech Results

Vodka, pickle juice, kettlebell lifting,and other Russian pastimes

'The working class sport'

Finally: Xtreme all around fitness!
Why Soviet science considers kettlebells to be one of the best tools for all around physical development....

Kettlebells in the Red Army
The Red Army catches on.... every Russian military unit equipped with K-bells....the perfect physical conditioning for military personnel....the vital combination of strength and endurance....*Girevoy sport* delivers unparalleled cardio benefits....why *Spetznaz* personnel owe much of their wiry strength, explosive agility, and stamina to kettlebells....

Section Two
Special Applications—How The Russian Kettlebell Can Dramatically Enhance Your Chosen Endeavor

Kettlebells for combat sports
Russian wrestlers do lion's share of conditioning with kettlebells.... Why KB one arm snatches work better than Hindu squats....KB's strengthen respiratory muscles.... boxers appreciate newfound ability to keep on punching....KB's reduce shoulder injuries.... develop the ability to absorb ballistic shocks....build serious tendons and ligaments in wrists, elbows, shoulders, and back—with power to match....why kettlebell drills are better than plyometrics as a tool for developing power....KB's the tool of choice for rough sports.

Why Russian lifters train with kettlebells
Famous Soviet weightlifters start Olympic careers with KB's.... Olympic weightlifters add KB's for spectacular gains in shoulder and hip flexibility.... for developing quickness.... overhead kettlebell squats unmatchable in promoting hip and lower back flexibility for powerlifters....

Get huge with kettlebells—if you wish
Why the *girya* is superior to the dumbbell or barbell, for arm and chest training....how to gain muscle size doing KB J&J's.... repetition one arm snatches for bulking up your back, shoulders, and biceps.... incorporating KB's into drop sets—for greater mass and vascularity.

Kettlebells for arm-wrestlers
World champion arm wrestler gives KB's two thumbs up....why the kettlebell is one of the best grip and forearm developers in existence....

Getting younger and healthier with kettlebells
The amazing health benefits of KB training....Doctor Krayevskiy's 20-year age-reversal....successful rehabilitation of hopeless back injuries with kettlebells.... Valentin Dikul—from broken back to All Time Historic Deadlift of 460kg, thanks to KB's.... why KB's can be highly beneficial for your joints.

How kettlebells melt fat and build a powerful heart—without the dishonor of dieting and aerobics
Spectacular fat loss....enhanced metabolism....increased growth hormone....a remarkable decrease in heart rates....

Section Three
Doing It—Kettlebell Techniques and Programs for Xtreme Fitness

Why Kettlebells?
The many reasons to choose K-bells over mainstream equipment and methods.... KBs suitable for men and women young and old.... perfect for military, law enforcement and athletic teams.... *Giryas*—a 'working class' answer to weightlifting and plyometrics promoting shoulder and hip flexibility....best bet for building best-at-show muscles.... highly effective for strengthening the connective tissues....fixing bad backs....cheap and virtually indestructible....promotes genuine 'all-around fitness' —strength, explosiveness, flexibility, endurance, and fat loss.

The program minimum

The Russian Kettlebell Challenge workout: the program-maximum
Pavel's own free style program....the top ten Russian Kettlebell Challenge training guidelines....how often and how long to train.... The secret key to successful frequent training.... THE most effective tool of strength development....difficulty and intensity variation.... how to add *Power to the People!* and other drills to your kettlebell regimen

The kettlebell drills: *Explode!*
- **Swing/snatch pull**
- **Clean**—The key to efficient and painless shock absorption.... making the clean tougher....the pure evil of the two K-bells clean.... seated hang cleans, for gorilla traps and shoulders....
- **Snatch** —The one-arm snatch—Tsar of kettlebell lifts
- **Under the leg pass** —A favorite of the Russian military—great for the midsection.
- **Jerk, Clean & Jerk**
- **Jump shrug**

The kettlebell drills: *Grind!*
- **Military press**—How to add and maximize tension for greater power....One hundred ways to cook the military press ... The negative press....the 'powerlifter's secret weapon for maximal results in your lifts....why to lift what you can't lift.... the graduated press....how to get more out of a 'light' weight.... the two-kettlebells press.... technique for building strength and muscle mass...the 'waiter press' for strict and perfect pressing skill....
- **Floor pullover and press**
- **Good morning stretch**—Favored by Russian weightlifters, for spectacular hamstring flexibility and hip strength.
- **Windmill**—An unreal drill for a powerful and flexible waist, back, and hips.
- **Side press**—A potent mix of the windmill and the military press—"one of the best builders of the shoulders and upper back."
- **Bent press** —A favorite lift of Eugene Sandow's—and The Evil One.... why the best-built men in history have been bent pressers....leads to proficiency in all other lifts....how to simultaneously use every muscle in your body.... A Brazilian Jiu Jitsu champion's personal kettlebell program

Section Four
Classic Kettlebell Programs from Mother Russia
The official Soviet weightlifting textbook *girevoy sport* system of training

The *Weightlifting Yearbook girevoy sport* programs

Three official armed forces *girevoy sport* programs

Group training with kettlebells—Red Army style

Xtreme kettlebell training—Russian Navy SEAL style
Performing snatches and other explosive kettlebell drills under water....pseudo-isokinetic resistance.... how to make your muscle fibers blast into action faster than ever....

"New Ab Machine Exposes Frauds, Fakes and Cheaters—But Rewards Faithful with the Most Spectacular Abs This Side of Heaven"

The Ab Pavelizer™ II
Item # P12

$130.00
10-25 lb Olympic plate required for correct use.
(You will need to supply your own plate)

#P12

NEW ITEM!

You know, it's a crying shame to cheat on your abs. Your abs are your very core, your center. Your abs define you, man or woman. So why betray them with neglect and less-than-honest carryings-on? That's bad! And everybody always knows! Rationalize all you want, hide all you want, but weak, flabby abs scream your lack of self-respect to all comers. Why live at all, if you can't hold your head up high and own a flat stomach?

Fortunately, you can now come clean, get honest and give your abs the most challenging, yet rewarding workout of their lives. And believe me, they will love you for ever!

Maybe you've been misled. Maybe you think you have to flog out hundreds of situps to get spectacular abs? Ho! Sorry, **but with abs, repetition is the mother of insanity.** Forget about it! You're just wasting your time! You're just fooling around! No wonder you're still not satisfied!

No, if you <u>really, really</u> want abs-to-die-for then: INTENSITY IS EVERYTHING!

FREE BONUS:

Comes with a four page detailed instruction guide on how to use and get the most out of your Ab Pavelizer™ II. Includes two incredible methods for massively intensifying your ab workout with *Power* and *Paradox Breathing*.

And here lies the secret of **The Ab Pavelizer™ II.** It's all in the extreme, unavoidable intensity it thrusts on you. No room for skulkers or shirkers. No room at all! Either get with the program or slink back under the stone from under which you crept.

You see, The Ab Pavelizer™ II's new sleek-'n-light design guarantees a perfect sit-up by forcing you to do it right. Now, escape or half-measures are impossible. Sit down at the Ab Pavelizer™ II and a divine slab of abs will be served up whether you like it or not. You'll startle yourself in your own mirror!

The secret to the Ab Pavelizer™ II is in the extra-active resistance it provides you. The cunning device literally pushes up against your calves (you'd almost swear it was a cruel, human partner) and forces you to recruit your glutes and hamstrings.

Two wonderful and amazing things happen.

First, it is virtually impossible to do the Janda situp wrong unless you start with a jerk. Second, the exercise becomes MUCH harder than on the Ab Pavelizer™ Classic. And "Much Harder" is Russian for "Quicker Results."

It is astonishingly hard to sit up all the way when the new Ab Pavelizer™ II is loaded with enough weight, 10-35 pounds for most comrades. If you can do three sets of five reps you will already have awesome abs.

A Great Added Benefit: Are you living in an already over-cluttered space? Want to conveniently hide the secret of your abs-success from envious neighbors? The new Ab Pavelizer™ easily and quickly folds away in a closet or under your bed. Once prying eyes have left, you can put it up again in seconds for another handshake with heaven—or hell, depending on your perspective.

1•800•899•5111 24 HOURS A DAY, OR FAX: (866) 280-7619

Join the Strength Elite For Ever— When You Own the *Rolls Royce* of Ab Machines

Introducing the Ab Pavelizer— the fastest, safest way to a ripped powerhouse of six-pack muscle

Bungee cords make it easier for beginners

Fits easily under the door

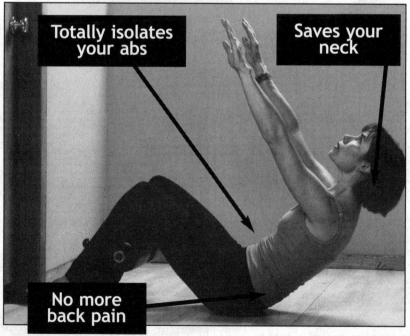

Totally isolates your abs

Saves your neck

No more back pain

In his groundbreaking book *Bullet-Proof Abs*—and in the new companion video— Russian Special Forces conditioning coach **Pavel Tsatsouline** reveals the Janda situp, the world's safest and most effective situp. Leading back and muscle function expert, Professor Janda discovered the secret to true ab strength—how to scientifically isolate the abs by "taking out" the hip flexors.

The result: an awesome exercise that scorches the abs, while avoiding the spine-wrecking, neck-jerking antics of traditional (read: outmoded) situps.

Until now, the Janda situp required a partner, for correct form. But with the introduction of the **Ab Pavelizer**, you can quickly develop world-class abs without having to rely on a friend. Now it's strictly between you and your abs. In just a few minutes a day, you can own the world—**ABSOLUTELY**.

The *Rolls Royce* of Ab Machines, you say? Well, more like the unholy union of a Humvee and a Rolls. Scary thought! Perhaps there should be a law against it. You get brutally rugged, all-terrain durability that'll stand a lifetime pounding from the most berserk of fitness freaks. Then there's the smooth-as-smoke, gloss powder coat finish that makes you just wanna stroke and caress the goddarn beauty of the thing.
Strong abs are the core, the very foundation of your power—why risk your success and future health with some flimsy, cheapo abs-toy? You deserve better. *You deserve the best*—get it today! And say goodbye forever to flabby abbies.

To Take Possession of Your New Abs Call This Number Immediately: 1-800-899-5111

"It Has Never Been So Easy to Have UNGODLY ABS"

Item # P9 The Ab Pavelizer
$170.00

1.

1. The Ab Pavelizer easily fits under a door, allowing you to perform a partner-free Janda sit up.

NOTE: Each Ab Pavelizer comes with "under door" attachability, Olympic plate adapter, bungee cord and handles.

2. Slide on a simple attachment (included), when you want to stabilize your Ab Pavelizer with a thirty-to-fifty pound Olympic plate. (You will need to supply your own plate)

2.

3.

3. The Ab Pavelizer, ready to use with an Olympic plate. Note the accompanying bungee cord, for those who need the extra help initially.

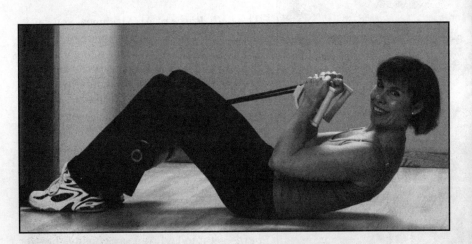

Testimonial Comments

"I have seen many abdominal routines in the last 25 years and the *Beyond Crunches* program is the best yet."—**Steve Maxwell, M.Sc., Senior World Brazilian Jujitsu Champion**

"The Russians are years ahead of us when it comes to training...Pavel is the man!" —**Todd Steussie, Minnesota Vikings**

"I learned a lot from Pavel's books and video, and plan to use many of his ideas in my own workouts, especially the nontraditional ab exercises described in *Beyond Crunches*— **Clarence Bass, author of Ripped 1, 2 & 3.**

"As a world record holding powerlifter, I know the importance of strong abs on maximum power performance. *Beyond Crunches* is THE text and authority on ab/trunk stability" — **Dr. Fred Clary, National Powerlifting Champion and World Record Holder.**

Beyond Crunches
Hard Science. Hard Abs.

With Pavel Tsatsouline
★★★★★

Featuring the Ab Pavelizer™
and the Fastest Way to
Bullet-Proof Abs

#V90

BEYOND CRUNCHES

By Pavel Tsatsouline
Video, Running time: 37 min
$29.95   #V90

"An Iron Curtain Has Descended Across Your Abs"

Possess a maximum impact training tool for the world's most effective abs, no question. Includes detailed follow-along instructions on how to perform most of the exercises described in the companion book, *Bullet-Proof Abs* Demonstrates advanced techniques for optimizing results with the Ab Pavelizer.

As a former Soviet Union Special Forces conditioning coach, **Pavel Tsatsouline** already knew a thing or two about how to create bullet-stopping abs. Since then, he has combed the world to pry out this select group of primevally powerful ab exercises—guaranteed to yield the fastest, most effective results known to man.

• Fry your abs without the spine-wrecking, neck-jerking stress of traditional crunches.

• No one—but no one—has ever matched Bruce Lee's ripped-beyond-belief abs. What was his favorite exercise? Here it is. Now you can rip your own abs to eye-popping shreds and reclassify yourself as superhuman.

• Russian fighters used this drill, *The Full-Contact Twist*, to increase their striking power and toughen their midsections against blows. An awesome exercise for iron-clad obliques.

• Rapidly download extreme intensity into your situps—with explosive breathing secrets from Asian martial arts.

• Employ a little-known secret from East German research to radically strengthen your situp.

• Do the right thing with "the evil wheel", hit the afterburners and rocket from half-baked to fully-fried abs.

• "Mercy Me!" your obliques will scream when you torture them with the *Saxon Side Bend*.

• How and why to <u>never, never</u> be nice to your abs—and why they'll love you for it.

• A complete workout plan for optimizing your results from the Janda situp and other techniques.

(Right) Pavel's Ab-strengthening breath techniques will give you the power to explode a water bottle—but don't try this trick at home—if the extreme air-pressure whacks back into your lungs, instead of exploding the water bottle—you can end up very dead, which is a bummer for everyone.

(Left) Pavel demonstrates the Power Breathing technique *Bending the Fire* to develop an extra edge in your abs training.

Yes, I Want My Fried Abs NOW!— I'm Done Wasting My Time with Slow Burns and Half-Baked Results

As a former Soviet Union Special Forces conditioning coach, Pavel Tsatsouline already knew a thing or two about how to create bullet-stopping abs. Since then, he has combed the world to pry out this select group of primevally powerful ab exercises—guaranteed to yield the fastest, most effective results known to man.

According to Pavel, "Crunches belong on the junk pile of history, next to Communism. 'Feeling the burn' with high reps is a waste of time!" Save yourself countless hours of unrewarding, if not useless—if not damaging—toil. Get with the program. Make fast gains and achieve blistering, rock-hard abs now.

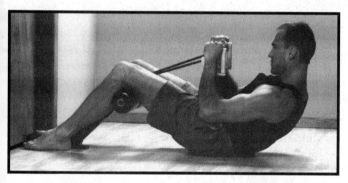

Fry your abs without the spine-wrecking, neck-jerking stress of traditional crunches—using this radical situp designed by the world's leading back and muscle function expert, Professor Janda, from Czechoslovakia.

When it came to wanting titanium abs yesterday, the Soviet Special Forces didn't believe in delayed gratification. Pavel gave them what they wanted. If you want abs that'll put you in the world's top 1 percent, this cruel and unusual drill does the trick.

No one—but no one—has ever matched Bruce Lee's ripped-beyond-belief abs. What was his favorite exercise? Here it is. Now you can rip your own abs to eye-popping shreds and reclassify yourself as superhuman.

Russian full contact fighters used this drill to pound their opponents with organ-rupturing power, while turning their own midsections into concrete.

1•800•899•5111
24 HOURS A DAY
FAX YOUR ORDER (866) 280-7619

Dragon Door

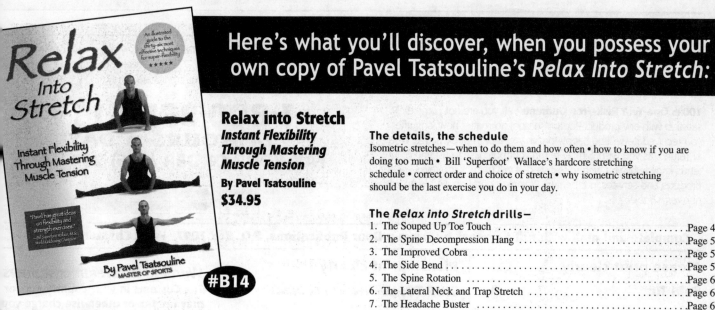

Here's what you'll discover, when you possess your own copy of Pavel Tsatsouline's *Relax Into Stretch:*

Relax into Stretch
Instant Flexibility Through Mastering Muscle Tension
By Pavel Tsatsouline
$34.95

#B14

tretching is **NOT** he best way to become flexible
Vhy Americans lose flexibility as they grow older • the dangers of physically tretching muscles and ligaments • *the role of antagonist passive insufficiency* • the nature and function of the *stretch reflex* • how to master muscular tension • ow to inhibit the stretch reflex • intensive and extensive learning methods.

Vaiting out the Tension— elaxed stretching as it should be
ust relax—when and when not to use the technique of *Waiting out the Tension* • Victor Popenko's key to mobility • the importance of visualization • why ear and anxiety reduce your flexibility • maximizing perceived safety in the retch.

Proprioceptive Neuromuscular Facilitation
low Kabat's PNF fools your stretch reflex • the function of the *Renshaw cell* why it works to pre-tense a stretched muscle.

Isometric stretching rules!
Vhy contract-relax stretching is 267% more effective than conventional relaxed retching • what the 'frozen shoulder' has to teach us • the lifestyle problem of ight weakness', • why isometrics is more practical than weights.

xtreme flexibility through *Contrast Breathing*
low to breathe your way to greater flexibility • effective visualizations for e tension/release sequence • avoiding the dangers of hyperventilation.

orced Relaxation— ie Russian spirit of stretching
low to turn the contract-relax approach into a thermonuclear stretching eapon • determining correct duration • tips for the correct release of tension.

he final frontier: why *Clasp Knife* stretches ill work when everything else fails
low to cancel out the *stretch reflex* • taking advantage of the *inverse retch reflex* • the last line of defense against injuries • shutdown reshold isometrics • mastering the Golgi tendon reflex.

hy you should not stretch your ligaments— nd how you can tell if you are
oga postures and stretches to avoid at all costs • the function and nitations of your ligaments.

tretching when injured
est, Ice, Compression and Elevation • what happens when a muscle gets jured • contracting and releasing the injury • why stretching won't help a d back and what to do instead.

he demographics of stretching
Vhy your age and sex should determine your stretches • the best—and orst—stretches for young girls, boys and adolescents • a warning for pregnant omen • what's best for older folks.

The details, the schedule
Isometric stretches—when to do them and how often • how to know if you are doing too much • Bill 'Superfoot' Wallace's hardcore stretching schedule • correct order and choice of stretch • why isometric stretching should be the last exercise you do in your day.

The *Relax into Stretch* drills—

How much flexibility do you really need?
Why excessive flexibility can be detrimental to athletic performance • why old school strongmen instinctively avoided stretching • what stretches powerlifters and weightlifters do and don't need • warning examples from sprinting, boxing and kickboxing.

When flexibility is hard to come by, build strength
Plateau-busting strategies for the chronically inflexible • *high total time under tension.*

Two more plateau busting strategies from the iron world
Popenko's flexibility data • the reminiscence effect • the dynamic stereotype • How to exceed your old limits with the stepwise progression.

Advanced Russian Drills for Extreme Flexibility—

ORDERING INFORMATION

Customer Service Questions? Please call us between 9:00am–11:00pm EST Monday to Friday at 1-800-899-5111. Local and foreign customers call 513-346-4160 for orders and customer service

100% One-Year Risk-Free Guarantee. If you are not completely satisfied with any product–for any reason, no matter how long after you received it–we'll be happy to give you a prompt exchange, credit, or refund, as you wish. Simply return your purchase to us, and please let us know why you were dissatisfied–it will help us to provide better products and services in the future. *Shipping and handling fees are non-refundable.*

Telephone Orders For faster service you may place your orders by calling Toll Free 24 hours a day, 7 days a week, 365 days per year. When you call, please have your credit card ready.

1·800·899·5111
24 HOURS A DAY
FAX YOUR ORDER (866) 280-7619

Complete and mail with full payment to: Dragon Door Publications, P.O. Box 1097, West Chester, OH 45071

Please print clearly

Sold To: **A**

Name_____

Street_____

City_____

State _____ Zip _____

Day phone*_____
* Important for clarifying questions on orders

Please print clearly

SHIP TO: *(Street address for delivery)*   **B**

Name_____

Street_____

City_____

State _____ Zip _____

Email_____

ITEM #	QTY.	ITEM DESCRIPTION	ITEM PRICE	A OR B	TOTAL

HANDLING AND SHIPPING CHARGES · NO COD'S
Total Amount of Order Add:

$00.00 to $24.99 add $5.00	$100.00 to $129.99 add $12.00
$25.00 to $39.99 add $6.00	$130.00 to $169.99 add $14.00
$40.00 to $59.99 add $7.00	$170.00 to $199.99 add $16.00
$60.00 to $99.99 add $10.00	$200.00 to $299.99 add $18.00
	$300.00 and up add $20.00

Canada & Mexico add $8.00. All other countries triple U.S. charges.

Total of Goods	
Shipping Charges	
Rush Charges	
Kettlebell Shipping Charges	
OH residents add 6% sales tax	
MN residents add 6.5% sales tax	
TOTAL ENCLOSED	

METHOD OF PAYMENT ☐ CHECK ☐ M.O. ☐ MASTERCARD ☐ VISA ☐ DISCOVER ☐ AMEX

Account No. *(Please indicate all the numbers on your credit card)*   EXPIRATION DATE

☐☐☐☐ ☐☐☐☐ ☐☐☐☐ ☐☐☐☐   ☐☐/☐☐

Day Phone ( ) _____

SIGNATURE _____ DATE _____

NOTE: We ship best method available for your delivery address. Foreign orders are sent by air. Credit card or International M.O. only. For rush processing of your order, add an additional $10.00 per address. Available on money order & charge card orders only.

Errors and omissions excepted. Prices subject to change without notice.

Warning to foreign customers
The Customs in your country may or may not tax or otherwise charge you an additional fee for goods you receive. Dragon Door Publications is charging you only for U.S. handling and international shipping. Dragon Door Publications is in no way responsible for any additional fees levied by Customs, the carrier or any other entity.

Warning!
This may be the last issue of the catalog you receive.

If we rented your name, or you haven't ordered in the last two years you may not hear from us again. If you wish to stay informed about products and services that can make a difference to your health and well-being, please indicate below.

Name_____

Address_____

City_____ State_____ Zip_____

Phone_____

Do You Have A Friend Who'd Like To Receive This Catalog?

We would be happy to send your friend a free copy. Make sure to print and complete in full:

Name_____

Address_____

City_____ State_____ Zip_____

DDP 06/02